Dark Side of North

Also by Anthony S. Abbott

Poetry
*The Girl in the Yellow Raincoat*
*A Small Thing Like a Breath*
*The Search for Wonder in the Cradle of the World*
*The Man Who*
*New and Selected Poems: 1989-2009*
*If Words Could Save Us*
*The Angel Dialogues*

Fiction
*Leaving Maggie Hope*
*The Three Great Secret Things*

Instruction
*What Writers Do*

Criticism
*Shaw and Christianity*
*The Vital Lie: Reality and Illusion in Modern Drama*

# Dark Side of North

poems

## Anthony S. Abbott

Press 53
Winston-Salem

Press 53, LLC
PO Box 30314
Winston-Salem, NC 27301

First Edition

Cover design by Claire V. Foxx

Cover image, "Full Moon Night by the Window in Summer,"
Copyright © 2017 by Rike, licensed through iStock

Author photo by Bill Giduz

Library of Congress Control Number
2020949669

Printed on acid-free paper
ISBN978-1-950413-31-7

To My Fellow North Carolina Writers

# Contents

# Foreword

(This foreword is adapted from the remembrance given on October 17, 2020, at Anthony (Tony) S. Abbott's memorial service.)

My name is Jacqueline Bussie, and Tony Abbott was my teacher. Speaking at Tony's funeral is the last assignment he ever gave me. I struggled fiercely with this final exam, as I fear it's one I truly cannot pass. I mean, what can you possibly say about the person to whom you owe your very self? In the end I decided that the only way to honor the sun-size light Tony was in my life is to share with you what he taught me. That way, I can let him do most of the talking. So here's my list of the top six things I learned from Tony Abbott.

## #1 Be a Lamp, a Ladder, and a Lifeboat

The poet Rumi once wrote, "Be a lamp, a ladder, and a lifeboat. Help someone's soul heal."[1] For Rumi, being these things for other people made your life count. Tony was one of those things to everyone who knew him. And for many really lucky people like me, Tony was all three. As you'll see in this book, Tony loved to give his poems titles that began with "The Man Who" or the "The Woman Who," like his poems "The Man Who Loved Trees" and "The Man Who Is Sorry." If Tony's life were a poem and I had to give it a title, I'd call it, "The Man Who was a Lamp, a Ladder, and a Lifeboat."

I had Tony for only one class at Davidson College, a class on religion and literature. I was a senior psychology major. I took the final exam in an unproctored room in Chambers. Suddenly, pen in hand, I found myself sobbing. Not because I was sad or doing poorly on the exam. No. The tears flowed because I came face-to-face with how much the class had changed me, helped me to grow, given me tools to help cope with the grief of losing my mom to early onset Alzheimer's. I cried because I realized I never wanted this class to end.

The next day, my roommate told me that Dr. Abbott had left a message on our answering machine saying I needed to go and see him about my final exam. I was terrified. Did he think I had cheated? Had I failed? I went to Tony's office. My bluebook lay open on the desk. "This exam," he said with genuine marvel in his voice, "this exam. Have you ever thought about going to divinity school, becoming a religion professor? Maybe going to Yale?" "No," I answered, "I'm a psych major . . . and I'm graduating in three days." "Well, you should consider it," he said. "You have a gift."

It's a cliché to say that one moment in your life changes everything, but in my case it's nonetheless true. When I came to Davidson, I was a first-generation college student. For people in my family, college was unnecessary, a PhD preposterous. I came to Davidson with little to no writing skills, many shameful prejudices and misperceptions, and absolutely no knowledge of what theology was or what college professors even did. But three years after my conversation that day with Tony, I did go to Yale. I did get a PhD in Religion and Literature. Today, I am a college professor, a theologian, and an author. Why? Because Tony Abbott's lamp shone on my shoulders. Because he took the time to call me and leave a message on my answering machine that day in May. You know, some people in life treat you as if you are just a drop in the ocean. But Tony treated me—and all of his students—as if we were the entire ocean in one drop.

For the next thirty years, Tony was my teacher, my friend, my mentor, and my adopted father, the dad I never had but always longed for. At Tony's seventieth birthday party he introduced me to everyone as his "adopted daughter." His words were hot glue that mended my Humpty-Dumpty heart. Aside from my mom, Tony was the person in my life who most wished me wings. Every day, I try to do the same for my own students.

### #2 Be Effluctress

When I was a nineteen-year-old student at Davidson, I played the clarinet in an orchestra concert that Tony attended. I remember looking up at the packed house in Davidson College Presbyterian Church and catching sight of Tony's face. His eyes twinkled, his hair stood on end from having removed his winter hat, and his face was filled with completely unmasked delight at our music. I mean the genuine kind of delight you rarely see on any adult's face. True story: I went home and wrote this observation in my journal, "I think Dr. Abbott has the secret to living. I want to figure out what it is."

Years later, I believe I did. Tony was effluctress. Tony wrote a splendid poem called "Effluctress," that he let me publish back in 2016 in my own book, *Outlaw Christian*. Effluctress is a word his friend Scott Owens' four-year-old daughter made up: it means a person who is able see the things four-year-old's see. The truth is, even when he was eighty-five, Tony Abbott, like all four-year-olds, was still wedded to wonder. "Learn again to take one step at a time toward the wonder," he once wrote in the poem "Seekers."[2] Tony saw, I mean really marveled at, things the rest of us grown-ups barely even notice anymore, like the song of a scarlet tanager, the smell of a rhododendron, the sight of a girl in a yellow raincoat.

Tony's favorite poet, Mary Oliver, once declared that paying attention is a form of prayer. Tony Abbott prayed aloud through his poems. Poetry was how Tony praised this marvelous and mutilated world. Mary Oliver also wrote, "When it's over, I want to say, all my life I was a bride married to amazement. I was the bridegroom, taking the world into my arms."[3] We all know Tony succeeded. He was married to amazement. His poems are the wedding ring of that lifelong union. Read them and become effluctress; take the world into your arms. Tony would want you to.

### #3 Remember That Everyone Wears the Sign

Every time I came to visit Tony, he'd ask me to speak at his church. One time after I taught his Sunday School class, several amazing humans came up and shared with me some very personal aspects of their own life story. Later, I said to Tony, "I don't know why it is, but that happens all the time: folks entrust me with their stories." Tony laughed and said, "You don't know why that is? I know why. It's because you wear the sign." "The sign?" I said, genuinely baffled. "What sign?" "The one around your neck, the one that I wear too," he replied. "The one that says, LOVE ME."

I've never forgotten that day. Tony taught me not to be afraid to wear the sign, and never to be ashamed of it. I grew up in a house of abuse, stoic secret-keeping, and toxic masculinity. I grew up afraid to express emotions, fearful to express love for fear I would be shot-down or worse, rejected. Tony taught me all of this was total life-crushing BS. As he reminds us in one of his poems, "If I had known is not enough. Say it now. Say it now. Say it now. Before the shutter clicks once more and closes."[4]

Tony had friends from all walks of life. He had friends who were in prison, friends who were millionaires, friends who were Republicans, friends who were Democrats, friends who were eighteen, friends who were eighty; friends who were poets, friends who were politicians. Watching how Tony lived, I learned that everyone—yes everyone, no exceptions—wears the sign, even if some people intentionally flip it around backwards.

## #4 Try like Humpty-Dumpty (to get put back together again)

Tony lived a beautiful and full life, that is for sure, but he wanted us to know it wasn't perfect. His childhood was filled with pain. Much like many of our own lives, his contained absence, alcoholism, loneliness, mother-loss, the loss of a child, and the experience of being forgotten. Suffering didn't make Tony unique. But what he did with it did.

Tony was the first adult, and the first teacher, I'd ever met in life who was willing to talk about the hard stuff. He taught us that suffering sucks. That suffering denied is suffering unhealed. He taught us to never sugarcoat suffering, smack a pink bow on it, or shove it to the back of the drawer. In one of my favorite lines in Tony's poetry, he urges us to get down to "the Humpty-Dumpty business of trying to make a jewel out of the cracked pieces of the heart."[5]

In these lines I discovered another part of Tony's secret of living. Tony composed his pain. He taught me this is possible. He taught me to be honest, to admit that this world is filled with turds and trash, yes it is. But he also taught me this: the totally wild thing about turds and trash is, they make incredible compost. Tony taught me that while pain should never be buried, denied, hidden, or sugarcoated, it can always be composted.[6]

It's beautiful to me that Tony was a consummate composter, married his whole life to his wife Susan, who is a consummate gardener. To me the deepest thing the two of them had in common during their sixty years together is this: in spite of everything, they both knew how to make life flower.

Our hearts are cracked open by Tony's death. But together, and only together, we can get down to the Humpty-Dumpty business of making that jewel.

## #5 Live like You are a Fucking Miracle

As I've said, I don't come from a functional family. Mine was marked with many of the same losses as Tony's own. One thing all the men in my family told me growing up, repeatedly, was that women did not need to go to college. I was so lucky to get a scholarship to go to Davidson, and to find a lifeboat-mentor there in Tony . . . who not only believed I belonged there, but that I should continue on to get a PhD. No one in my life had ever believed in me like that before.

Over the years, I shared with Tony painful stories about my family life. Tony gave the homily at my wedding, and unfortunately, at that event, he witnessed some of my family's painful dysfunction on full display. I'll never forget the conversation we had afterward. Tony didn't criticize my family or make me feel ashamed. Instead, he looked straight at me and declared, "Jacqueline Bussie, you are a fucking miracle." He then laughed that spectacular laugh of his. That laugh that carbonated the air of any room. And I laughed too. But the truth is, Tony was a fucking miracle too. The truth is, you are a fucking miracle, and Tony would want you to remember that.

## #6 Claim Joy as Your Birthright

During the pandemic summer of 2020, I helped Tony edit and arrange his book, *Dark Side of North*. Reading it broke my heart and stitched it back together all at the same time. It is undeniably a dying poet's last gift to us. In the book's final poem called "The Last," Tony begs us "to receive every morning as a wrapped gift." Tony did this. He lived, loved, and sought joy the way he drove his car—not dangerously, but fiercely, and definitely over the speed limit.

Tony dined out on delight—delight in his family, his students, his teaching, sunsets over Lake Norman, a well-made gin and tonic. He taught me and all of his students to claim joy as our God-given birthright. To wait for it to show up. As he observes in one of his poems, "If I sit long enough without speaking, I begin to believe that God will walk in the door like cream rising to the top. I wait for God to enter—I watch for signs."[7]

Tony's colleague, Karl Plank, shared the most stunning story about joy and Tony. Once Tony visited Karl's religion class. Karl was teaching Jesus' treasure parable, and emphasized to the students the need to give up everything to follow Jesus. But Karl forgot to mention a key phrase from the scripture. The man in the parable who gives everything up, does so in joy. From the back of the classroom, it was Tony who reminded

Karl what he had forgotten. Grinning, Tony asked, "But what about the joy, Karl, what about the joy?"

In another poem called "Do Not Forget This," Tony shares what, in the end, he most wanted to remember about his life, and it is courageous advice for us all. "Each morning, when you awake, kneel down and place your forehead on the floor, the ground, the carpet, wherever you are. Give thanks for the life of your wife, give thanks for your sons. Speak their names one at a time each morning . . . Be thankful for the gift of life and the small birds who drink from the pool outside your window. Then rise and start the day."[9]

My name is Jacqueline Bussie, and those are the top six things I learned from my teacher, Tony Abbott. Let's always remember him as The Man Who Was a Lamp, a Ladder, and a Lifeboat to so so many. As The Man Who Was Effluctress. As The Man Who Wore the Sign and Remembered Everyone Else Wears It Too. Let's always remember him as The Man Who Tried Like Humpty-Dumpty. As The Man Who Never Forgot: We are All Fucking Miracles. As The Man Who Claimed Joy as His Birthright.

Dr. Jacqueline Bussie
October 17, 2020
Davidson, North Carolina

[1] Rumi, *The Big Red Book*, ed. Coleman Barks, "A Well-Baked Loaf," p. 295
[2] "Seekers," *The Girl in the Yellow Raincoat*, p. 37
[3] "When Death Comes," by Mary Oliver
[4] "Evening Light," *The Girl in the Yellow Raincoat*, p. 25
[5] "Before Forty," *The Girl in the Yellow Raincoat*, p. 63
[6] My appreciation for Tony's "secret to living" and learning to compost our pain appear in my book *Outlaw Christian: Finding Authentic Faith by Breaking the Rules* (Nelson Books: Nashville, 2016), pgs. 162-163, 182, 234-235
[7] "Not Wisely but Too Well," *The Girl in the Yellow Raincoat*, p. 22
[9] "Do Not Forget This," *Dark Side of North*, p.123

# Acknowledgments

How this book came to be written is an unusual story, which will give me the means of thanking the many people who helped me through the process.

*The Angel Dialogues* was published in 2014, and I thought it might be my final book of poems. I continued over the next four or five years to write individual poems, but I did not send them out, and the only poem published during that time was "In the Retirement Home," in *Kakalak 2016*. Then, in 2019, I had a thought: What about the poems in all my different computer files that had never been published? Maybe I should go back to them. And I did.

Combining the older poems with the newer ones, I found over one hundred pages of poems, and I set to work revising and editing the ones that needed work. In March of 2020, the Pines at Davidson, where I live, was fundamentally shut down and I found myself with much more time to work on poetry. So I took the hundred or so pages—which Cathy Barton, the Department of English Assistant, had put into a new file for me—and I sent them to two splendid poet friends, Claire Poulson and Marilyn Rousseau, and asked them to write Yes, No, or Maybe on each poem. I sent them four or five poems a day for three weeks, and at the end, we kept the Yes's, which I now had to organize into a book-length manuscript.

What happened was remarkable. I started putting the poems into piles, and they organized themselves into seven stacks, "books," I called each of them. Each book was complete in itself, a small volume of about fifteen pages, and the seven books made a unified manuscript about the last twenty years of life, and how we deal with diminishing health, retirement, changes in living, losses—how we maintain our joy for living in the midst of these challenges. My student assistant, Evelyn Schaeffer, working from home in Atlanta, put these seven books together in order, and I added at the beginning, the title poem, "Dark Side of North."

I then sent the manuscript to my friend Jacqueline Bussie, the Director of the Forum on Faith and Life at Concordia College, Minnesota, and she read the book carefully, suggesting the movement of some poems from one section to another, the reordering of some poems, and the elimination of a few. Her suggestions were brilliant, and now I had a book. . . .

Evelyn Schaeffer made all the changes in the manuscript, which I now sent to other poet friends just be sure I really had a book. Shawn Henry, Janet Sarjeant, and Janet Joyner all said that I did, and so I sent the manuscript to Kevin Watson at Press 53, who accepted it. Then I asked Joseph Bathanti, Shelby Stephenson, Jaki Shelton Green, Dannye Romine Powell, and Jacqueline Bussie to write blurbs. They all agreed. And that is how the book came to be put together.

As an expression of gratitude to these people for their support and hard work, I am dedicating this book "To My Fellow North Carolina Writers"—not only this specific group, but the many others whose kindness has sustained me over the years.

Anthony S. Abbott
August 2020
Davidson, North Carolina

*Prologue*

# Dark Side of North

The dark side of north, or is it the north
side of dark, looms strangely over
the upturned world. Hurricanes without
rain, tornadoes without wind
(yet the red buds blossom obscenely)

Times Square deserted except for two
Japanese tourists in masks. Restaurants, bars,
theaters, libraries all dark. Trucks with bodies
in the streets outside the hospitals
(red buds laugh in our shocked faces)

In Florida college students frolic on the beach.
Primaries postponed, churches, schools
learning to Zoom. Conferences cancelled.
Bath tissue shelves empty, but why?
(daffodils multiply like yellow square roots)

So stop, whoever you are, and look around you.
Perhaps I will be here, perhaps not. I am, they say,
among the most vulnerable. This is my remembrance.
I cannot touch you except with broken words
(azaleas pink and white quiver in the breeze)

We are on the dark side of north, the north side of dark.
Tens of thousands one doctor says. At the Bronx Zoo
even a tiger has tested positive for the virus.
Wipe the railings, wipe the doorknobs, wash your hands
(in Washington the cherry blossoms smile to the empty paths)

Perhaps you are reading this ten years from now
and I say to you we are like whales stranded on the beach.
We can sing from our balconies, but we cannot touch.
We die in tens, then hundreds, then thousands
(the crosses on the dogwood blossoms tremble in terror)

We wonder what there will be when we walk
once more on the open streets. What price the touch
of a friend, a grandchild? On Palm Sunday, the Pope spoke
alone to an empty St. Peter's Square. No cardinals
(the fingers of love beckon through the greening leaves).

# Part One

## *The Book of Remembrances and Grace*

# A Poem for My Daughter on Her Fiftieth Birthday

### 1.

The thing is, I miss you more than ever.
Even the old graveyard has lost its charm.
The trees forgot to turn this year. Where are
the blood reds, the succulent oranges?
Nothing there but tired yellow and dusty
graying green, nothing there but curled brown.

And you—remember when you sat
in the top of the maple tree talking to me—
and now you're gone. Have you danced away
like the girl in the book, to another
heaven far beyond the blue call
of us tired earthfolk.

### 2.

Remember the time at the barbershop
how you stuck your head in the open door.
"Nice haircut," you said. The barber whisked me
with his broom. "Nice shirt," you said, and we walked
hand in hand all the way to the graveyard.
The stone marker was our table. You sat
at the head, and Jesus, of course, at the foot.

We drank the wine, one at a time, and munched
the bread. I woke in the barber chair
as if you were never there, and stepped
into the April sun slanting through the new leaves,
wine stains on my shirt, a small piece
of earthen bread caught between my fingers.

### 3.

Yesterday I parked the car behind
the Post Office and listened to the end
of Beethoven's Fifth. I couldn't bear to let
it finish without me. I hear the notes
as if for the first time, the pure Platonic
form of the notes, the essence of musicness.

I will you beside me. I pray your presence
into being, you at fifty, fully formed,
body and soul woven as one.


4.

I sit in the car by the graveyard, looking at
the beautiful Christmas wreath. I hate to take
it down, but it's past New Years, and we must,
they all tell us, move on. Sweet Jesus, move on,
to what? They've got me in the old folks' home,
hung up among the walkers and the bent
bodies. We learn to make do among ourselves,
tickle the fancy with light games and the taste
of good wine. It's a pleasant kind of death.

On the other side of the street the children
walk into the school. They are moving on.
And I, I still have my eye open for you. I put
the wreath in the back seat. Tomorrow I will
volunteer at the school. Perhaps I will see you there.

# Lyn's Poem

All morning I have thought of you
the long vowels like the stretch of years
since you slipped into that strange darkness
at the top of the stairs, slipped away and
hovered in the bridges of my mind
like ropes over a dark water. And now

finally I know I had it wrong, or at least
had it sideways, missing the sweet heart
at the center. It was never about the losing,
only the having. And I didn't know that
until my angel told me. Write about
the luck, she said, write about the luck.

I loved you even before you were born.
I wanted you so much. When the doctor
said it's a girl with some edge of dismay
in his gravel voice, I could have hit him.
I wanted you, and I got you. You were perfect.
That's all there is to say—except this—

you did it all before you left. That's what
I see now. You took your brother up the stairs
and played for hours without us hearing you.
You taught him love and grace and quietness
which he carries to this day. You knew something
the rest of us did not.

I don't know. I forget things. The years muddy
the memory. I had been away—all summer almost.
Something it was that led me round the back,
and there you were alone, in the sandbox playing
by yourself, quietly, peacefully, of course. I called
across the lawn—and you looked up, and then
you came to me. "Da," you said, and again, "Da,"
and hooked your legs around my waist, your arms
around my neck. I carried you in the house.

On Easter Sunday, the day before you died,
you held the neighbor's baby in your arms.
Later your grandfather held you. "She would
never let me hold her before," he said. "She
only wanted Dad." I understood that for four
years you gave yourself to me, and then you left
like an April snow. Tell about the luck, my angel
said. So here it is. You came perfect, you left
perfect. Is this a love poem? Yes....

# Third from the Left

The boy in the back row, third from the left
with the cowlick and the lock of brown hair
down his forehead. Look at his eyes and how
they say almost to the camera itself,
"Please love me." Here I am setting up
with the big black cloth over my head
watching them all, pushing, jostling, shoving,
poking, grinning—but not this one. He just
stands there looking into the lens with those
dark, dark eyes. I tell you, he's been somewhere,
that one, seen some things the others haven't.
He won't talk about them, though. No sir.
Not him. He's a silent one. And the others?
They don't mess with him. They respect him.
Or they fear him, I don't know which. He wants
something they don't know about yet. Those boys,
the rest of them, would laugh if he said "love"
to them. So he won't, no, he won't and there's
no one else to talk to but the teachers
and you know a boy won't say love to them.

He's doomed, that one. He'll find it where he can
and some of the places won't be so good.
He'll take a stick of peppermint and think
it's paradise. The world knows how to hurt—
he'll take his lumps, all right. But if he ever
finds the thing itself, then watch out, He's
a deep one. All that stuff inside pouring out
to some poor girl who thought to be nice—
she'll have her hands full. And if she's smart
and if she's brave and fool enough, she'll
keep him. Those eyes, my God, those eyes.

# The Man Who Played Frederick

I was talking to the ninth graders
at my old boarding school.
"What was your favorite time in your
childhood?" one student asked.

Something at school, surely, I think,
but I can't remember what.
This morning, driving to Anson County
to teach at a conference, I play

*The Pirates of Penzance* in the car.
I sing all the songs, with great joy.
I pound on the steering wheel
like the great bass drum. "I am

a Pirate King," I sing, and then
mouth the multisyllables of the
Modern Major General. My God,
I think, of course that is the answer.

When Dorothy Wheeler, the sexy
music teacher whose breasts we loved
to peek at when she bent to put
a record on, when Dorothy Wheeler,

bless her, asked me to play Frederick
in *Pirates of Penzance*, when Dorothy
Wheeler, bless her, changed the score
because my voice was changing

and I couldn't reach the high notes
anymore. Oh how I loved that play.
Tonight, I drive home to the lake
and I sing the songs again, over
and over. At the end, I kissed
the boy who played Mabel
(there were no girls at this school)
and the whole audience roared

and Mrs. Wheeler smiled at me
and blew me a kiss. How could I
have forgotten that?

# What the Prefects Would Never Know

His parents were coming to take him home,
and he had walked back to his room to pack
his things. By lunchtime he would be gone,
and in a few months the boys would forget
about him. From his window he gazed
at the river one last time.
                              For a while
they would all talk about how they
had dragged him down the hall, naked,
to the showers and thrown him in. How
they had made him scrub himself hard
with rough soap that stung his skin
and made him zig zag back to his room
between the lines of laughing students
who flicked their towels at him and laughed
like chimpanzees.
                              They would not know
what this had cost him. They would not know
why he had lived among them for so many
weeks without uncovering himself, why
he could not bear their rude laughter, their jeers,
their silly apish playing with themselves.
He was not one of them and would never be,
but he loved the smooth river flowing by
and the click of the oars as the crew shells
made their way along in perfect rhythm.

# The Boy from Somwehere Else

lived in the open mouth of the world.
He chewed on the dry branches of time.
He was handsome enough, to be sure,

but there was in his voice
the deep well of absence.
He was with them, but not of them.

His speech was familiar, but not theirs,
and when he told tales
of his drunken uncles and stage-struck

sisters, they nodded politely
and they spoke in their apple-round voices
of kith and kin, and told how their

grandfathers had founded the first
bank in Hitchcock County.
He would wait, this boy.

He would find one day the person
who could hear his music
as blood red leaves matched autumn.

He could not be mistaken about this.
When she came, he would recognize her
at once—as one knows the coming storm

by the first, distant clap of thunder.
Perhaps he could not keep her.
Perhaps one can never keep such a gift.

But, still, she would grace his years—the buds
of his growing up, the rattling trains of the
middle passage, the brittle bones of the slow

descent, the icy nights of the final coming down.

# All Saints' Day

Sunday morning, and after last night's rain
the robes of the saints cover the green grass.
Next to the church—in the naked branches
of the trees the sound of humming, the whirr

of wings. The remains of the demons' night
lie scattered everywhere, torn masks grinning
like drunken devils, white sheets in the
bramble bushes behind the old manse.

I think the saints are the spiders of the soul.
They spin their webs around us and wait
to catch us unawares. Flowers on my
mother's grave—in my mind she rises.

I hear the blues piano of her youth
and the smile she gave the men when she played.
You see, I never knew her really, never
sought to find the anchor of her soul.

What was her voice like, I ask. I do
not know. The last time I heard it was sixty
years ago. Was it soft and musical
like the lilt of her Georgia childhood?

Did she leave me something I have not yet
discovered, some letter written but never
delivered? Did she leave her cloak on the
ground with the capes of the other saints?

Was her color red? The whirr of wings sends
me upward in the search. The woman in
the blue gown beckons. She smiles darkly
but the wind says wait. Next year is soon

enough, when the saints gather again
at the foot of the old tree next to the
church and take off their shoes and rest.
Listen, the wind says, listen and wait.

# Muddle

My mother says she is in a muddle.
"Middle," I say. "You mean middle."
"The world's a muddle," she says.
"True enough," I say, "but you are
in a middle." "How's that?" she asks.

"Do you feel pain? Do you feel grief?"
"No," she says, wiping her lower lip
with a red plaid napkin. "And do you feel
joy, do you feel ecstasy?" "No," she says.
"My bureau is neat. A place for every item."

"Yes," I say. "At night he comes back,"
she says, "but I do not see him."
"No tears," I say. "No tears," she says.
"Tears are too sad." "Joy, too," I say.
"Ah well," she says. "I told you."

"No tears in the writer, no tears
in the reader," I say. "Ah," she says,
"'tis a muddle indeed.'"

# Lost and Found

For a moment I will try
  to plant the orchid
    of your mother's life
      in the soil of these slant sounds.

She blossomed
  she spread the sun
    of her sweet warmth
      among the rest of us.

We grew too. You most
  of all. You knew what
    a mother was and your
      heart spoke truths

into her giving ear
  week after month after
    clanging day. She answered
      back with a wand of faith.

All that is forever there.
  The cuts, the bruises healed
    the soul restored. The past
      is inviolable.

For a moment only
  you are lost. We are
    all lost. But do not fear.
      It all comes back again

in ways we cannot know.
  You will be she, and
    your daughter will be you.
      You will hear her love

filled words from your
   own mouth, and your words
      coming back to you from
         the growing woman you have made.

What she gave you
   you take inside
      and cultivate like growing seed.
         You walk into a room

and transfix the ordinary
   with your hidden life
      the life she gave you day by day
         for all her years.

Her gift shines in the night sky
   and the softness of the spring rain.
      You carry it well.
         No, more than well. Beautifully

# Even the Grass

In memory of Robert Whitton

Even the grass misses you. I think
of the walk you took every day, the steps
from your house to the college and back,
the steps on the rough sidewalk
over the hallowed crossing
to the campus itself, blooming in the spring
with the dark crosses of dogwood, with astonishing
azaleas. The grass received your steps every day.
Perhaps you stopped and sat on the stone bench
and looked up at the turning leaves in the fall,
and thought for a time about the people you had blessed.

Saw them among the leaves, the students, who never
grew old, coming year after year, night after night, and how
that night you walked home for the last time
you must have been thinking of one of them
as you crossed the street.

I like to think of you in the middle of the day, your work
spread out on one of the round Union tables—your
office—and how you could take the mysteries of calculus
and make them clear to all who asked.

You are here among us, your steps keeping pace
with ours, your laughter echoing off the walls
of our offices, where sometimes, on Friday afternoons,
there was time for a glass of sherry and easy words
among friends.

You are here at Summit, smiling among the others
at Kate Minogue and her sweet round voice,
but not as good as Emmylou Harris with her
perfect cheekbones. You are standing
ankle deep in a cold mountain stream
looking for your missing lens so you could see again.
You are here on Sunday evenings in your dining room
laughing with Amy among the lucky guests. You are
in Pittsburgh telling your friends you want
to go down a coal mine.

I see you in the fading light of evening
sky pink in the west, walking toward us,
walking home toward us all, telling us
to live.

*Davidson, NC*
*December 6, 2011*

# Last Word

In memory of Joseph Bacon Martin III

He was always wiser than the rest of us.
Trapped in the unwanted cocoon of his
useless body, his mind knew oceans
of worlds. Once when we almost lost him,
he came back. It was, he said, spelling out
the letters on his clear plastic board,
the most beautiful world he'd ever seen.
He'd struggled to return to us. Next time
he might not. He spelled the name of the place
with his eyes. P-E-A-C-E. Twice he repeated it.

When the end came, his wife sat up with him
all night. She knew something was wrong.
She could not make him comfortable.
With his eyes he told her he was cold.
She pulled the blanket up. He asked the time,
then asked her with those eyes to stay awake.
He asked the time again, and yet again.
Morning approached. She opened up the blinds,
let in the light. In the silence of dawn,
he looked at the lake. "Get Rusty," the eyes said.
He'll be here soon, she answered.

He tried to speak. "P" he spelled out to her,
then a letter she could not understand.
Then A-C-E. Once more he spoke
and she tried to catch his eyes, but the eyes
were going. In the driveway, the sound
of Rusty's car. The eyes closed. He had
spoken his final word.

# The Leaving

Nothing left now but the memory itself,
the event fading even as he thinks
of it—the plane gliding to earth
in snow covered Salt Lake City, white
everywhere, then off again and Mount Rainier
rising as if by magic toward
the left wing, then the sea itself,
the blue Pacific, the long car ride
and the ferry, humming smooth as a cello's
strokes toward the islands and finally
the sun setting when it docks at the harbor.

And then she is there, the beloved sister,
still herself, lying in the bed Hospice
has made, lifting her arms toward him, bringing
him down close, still her baby brother after
all these years. He tells her she was a good
mother to him when they were young. She smiles
and sighs relief. She worried she had failed him,
She tires. The nurses ready her for sleep.

In the morning he rises with the sun
to say his love. Her arms lift to encircle him.
He lowers his head, and she kisses him
with open mouth. "My Dickie, my love,"
she murmurs sweetly. "Your brother," he laughs,
"your baby brother." "I thought you were my Dickie,"
she says. "I know," he answers. "But where is
my Dickie?" she asks. "Dickie will be here soon," he says.

She would follow her Dickie anywhere, even
to death itself. She nods off, wakes, he tells her
once again she was a good mother to him
when things were bad at home. He holds
her hand until she sleeps.

He walks outside and looks toward the ocean.
Tomorrow he will fly home. She will die, a week
later, on his birthday.

# The Light in the Window

In memory of Nancy Abbott Hieronymus (1926-2017)

How early I must have known that she was
my true mother, that when she packed her bag
I must go with her. She would keep me safe.

How early I must have known that she was
my true teacher, making the sounds of the words
with her mouth so I could learn them, too.

How early I must have known that she was
my true protector, throwing herself across me
slashing her knee on the broken windshield glass.

Later, when I was nearly grown, cocky sophomore
in prep school, riding the subway home at 2 a.m.,
she left a light in the window on that I

would turn out when I came in. I didn't know
she stayed awake until she heard the door open
and close, heard the click of the light going off.

Now I sit by her bed and watch her sleep and wake,
sleep and wake, and tell me how she loves
her precious Dick, how she will hold his hand

all the way to heaven. Beyond the light in her window
the evening comes over the island, the deer prick up
their ears, the foxes peek from their dens. In the pines

the gold crowned kinglet waits. She is coming, they say,
our friend is coming, the one who loved us all these years.
Tonight I will go home, and the friends who loved her so

will arrive, one by one, to take her in their arms,
and the next night the angel will stand at the foot
of her bed. You are loved, he will say, and enfold her

with his bright wings. And she will go where that brightness
is and, like a light in the window, shine upon us all.

# Sophie's Choice

I read the book in the quiet of my room
you saw the movie in downtown Greensboro
I had not seen the movie
you had not read the book.

You saw the movie in downtown Greensboro
you did not know what was going to happen
you had not read the book
You were only eighteen. Your heart was pure.

You did not know what was going to happen
neither did I. I suspected nothing
you were eighteen, your heart was pure
I was forty-seven, the middle of my life.

I suspected nothing when I came to the page
I came to Sophie's choice and froze
I was forty-seven, the middle of my life
I hurled the book across the room.

I came to Sophie's choice and froze
you saw her choice from your theatre seat
I hurled the book across the room
you stood and ran to the theatre door.

You saw her choice from your theatre seat
your heart beat hard in disbelief
you stood and ran to the theatre door
On a lobby bench you cried and cried.

Your heart beat hard in unbelief
you never saw the film's sad end
on a lobby bench you cried and cried
didn't know how Sophie and Nathan died.

You never saw the film's sad end
I picked the book up off the floor.
you didn't know how Sophie and Nathan died
my glass angel shattered in its fall.

I picked the book up off the floor
and read and read deep into the night
my glass angel had shattered in its fall
I read to find some hope, some meaning to it all.

I read and read deep into the night.
You scream to God—how could such people be?
I read to find some hope, some meaning
you ache for the lost leaf of faith

you scream to God—how could such people be?
You put the book away for thirty years
you ache for the lost leaf of faith
and now I place my copy in your hands

you put the book away for thirty years
memories of the movie fade in time
and now I place my copy in your hands
which you will read, in the quiet of your room.

# Instructions

Park the car in the elementary school.
Cross the street to the little league field,
turn right and walk past the first base dugout.
Think of the boys in there buzzing—batter,
batter, batter. Keep walking and follow the outfield
fence all the way to the cemetery. Keep turning
to the left until you come to the exact center.

Look toward home plate, and imagine yourself
a ball hit by a strong young man, imagine
the ball flying over your head and rolling,
rolling, rolling, then coming to rest by a small
gray marker. Turn and follow the ball, or, if you like,
follow the headstones—Thomas, Farmer, Peele.

You will come to an open space and see—some
God awful plastic flowers decorating her grave.
I'm afraid to take them away. They might have
some significance, don't you think?  No headstone.
Just space, space for me to lie next to her someday.

Kneel down and cut your knees on the letters
of her name. Close your eyes and speak to her.
She'll know you. Ask her how she is, or even
how it is up there, out there, wherever there is.

Maybe one can just go without knowing,
but I feel you know something that I don't.
If there's a God out there, she does. And well,
the two of you, that would be something else,
something grand. Something to die for.

# House Concert

For Gracie

Today she has come home.
For days she slept in the hospital
eyes closed, breathing ragged
but now she has opened her eyes.

For days she slept in the hospital
while her mother and father watched
but she opened those blue-grey eyes
and now she is breathing room air.

Her mother and father keep watch
as they tune their wooden instruments
now she is breathing room air
and she gazes at them once more.

They tune their wooden instruments
the sweet cello and the brave recorder
she gazes at them once more
as the sound of music fills the room.

The sweet cello and the brave recorder
join with the flutes and the harpsichord.
The sound of music fills the room
as she sits in the back and watches.

The flutes rejoice, the harpsichord dances,
the dog licks the hands of the seated guests
She sits in the back and watches
—her brother facebooks on his computer.

The dog licks the hands of the seated guests
—the small bones in the ear tingle with joy
her brother facebooks on his computer
her mother's feet tap with her bright red shoes.

The small bones in the ear tingle with joy
the full moon shifts in the evening sky
her mother's feet tap with her bright red shoes
as the cello sings her daughter back to life.

The full moon shifts in the evening sky.
Yesterday she lay asleep, eyes closed, breathing ragged
the cello sings the daughter back to life.
Today, dear Gracie, you have come home.

# Part Two

*The Book of Jesus*

# A Tailor Can Stitch a Suit of Clothes
## but Only God Can Stitch the Soul

The needle goes in twice
through the skin, like ice
or burning, one or the other.
If there were a mother
she would touch my lips
or even still me with a kiss
and say it only hurts once,
this stitch. I'm no dunce.
Yesterday I saw the moon
standing at half in the high noon.
Stitch one, says God, and smiles.
Stitch two, says Christ, and beguiles
me with his soft, high cry.
Stitch three, I do not lie,
the Holy Ghost roils it into me—
anything I want, anything, you see—
I'm stitched anew, now God wills
his breath, blowing, blowing fills
the leather pouch of me. I am His,
Hers, whose, no matter, there is
nothing now but to let the breath
come in and out, God's breath, death
no longer proud, no longer long
or deep, and no wrong
can harm, hurt, wound the deep
stitched soul which I can keep,
the deep stitched soul, the stitches
holding true, yes, the stitches
tight, holding the brightness in the eye
holding the blueness of the sky,
soul inviolate in the endless light
of the now surrendered, vanished night.

# Mary, Mother of God

Just before dawn
when the angel

flew away, as she does,
I slept again

and dreamed of stairs.
I climbed.

My leg hurt, as it does,
but I climbed

and at the top, there
you were

as I knew you
would be

because if you were not
there would have

been no point at all
in the climb.

You wore blue and
smiled

and beckoned to me
to come

but when I took
the next step

the stairs themselves
vanished

and I looked
out

into the night sky
searching

for some sign
of you.

But I saw only
the tips

of my beckoning
fingers.

# Strange New Jesus

I am reading once more the Gospel of John.
The rain pelts against the west windows.
His strange new Jesus stands before me.
I want to put the book away.

The rain pelts against the west windows.
He has seen all since the beginning of time.
I want to put the book away
This know-it-all Jesus frightens me.

He has seen all since the beginning of time.
He is one with the Father, the distant Father.
This know-it-all Jesus frightens me,
This Jesus whom even Pilate reveres.

He is one with the Father, the distant Father.
He knows the Father's will, no one else does,
This Jesus whom even Pilate reveres.
He turns the water into wine, he raises Lazarus.

He knows the Father's will, no one else does
If you believe in him, you are saved—
He turns the water into wine, he raises Lazarus
It is finished, he says at the end.

If you believe in him, you are saved—
This strange new Jesus stands before me.
It is finished he says at the end
I am reading the Gospel of John.

# The Writing on the Ground

*But Jesus stooped down, and with his finger wrote on the ground, as though he heard them not. So when they continued asking him, he lifted up himself, and said unto them, "He that is without sin among you, let him first cast a stone at her." And again he stooped down, and wrote on the ground.*

—John 8:6-8

I am paging through the Gospel of John,
in my Revised Standard Edition
and behold chapter eight begins with verse twelve.
Yes, verse twelve. The whole story of the woman
taken in adultery has vanished.
No Pharisees skulking away, afraid
to cast the first stone, no writing on the ground,
no moment of compassion from Jesus.

My heart is broken. I want it back.
I want to hear Jesus tell the woman
he does not condemn her. I want to see
the writing on the ground, the very words
he writes twice. Are they the same words?
Who sees them? Are they for the Pharisees,
to tell them something they do not know?

"Go thy way and sin no more," he says, and there
the story ends. But maybe not. Maybe she
says, "Go where?" She can't go home. Her husband
will kill her. The man she loved has disappeared.
What does Jesus know about women like her?
Maybe she says, "Go where?" and he writes
"God loves you" in the dirt—or something
to let her know her sin belonged not so much
to her, but to men.

# To Have Been There

*For this is the will of my Father, that everyone who sees the Son
and believes in him should have eternal life; and I will raise him
up at the last day.*
    —John 6:40

I have been thinking about eternal life,
about what happens when we die,
about what belief means. Somehow
before, it was less important.
I always used to say eternal life was

God's problem, not ours. It was all
a matter of grace. If you believed,
it was a gift. You couldn't control it.
You couldn't worry about it, you
couldn't make it happen.

Faith is God's business, that's what
I always used to say. Our business is to love.
But now it's bigger than that, more than that.
I can't grasp it. Here is Jesus, in Capernaum,
he's taken the boat from Tiberias, slipped

away, and the people, desperate to find him,
have climbed into their fishing boats and rowed,
sailed, I don't know, to Capernaum. And he
tells them that if they believe, they will have
eternal life. And the Pharisees murmured

against him, isn't that wonderful? Murmured.
And Jesus says, "Do not murmur among
yourselves." I love that. I can see the scene.
The Pharisees saying, this is Joseph,
the carpenter's son. How can he give eternal

life to anyone? But there it is, there it is.
Eternal life, for the grasping, the hand
reaching toward Jesus, touching him. I believe,
you say, I believe, because I want it so badly.

Wanting to live forever, here, there, wherever
there is life. To have it never stop. There is Jesus,
standing on the corner in his hometown,

the Pharisees murmuring, and the people,
that's the point, the people, staring,
mouths open, tears in their eyes. They have been
changed by this man who opens his mouth
and everything is different. Everything.

That's what eternal life is, that everything—
isn't it, that everything transformed
into light, into joy, into the love that needs
nothing more.

# The Kiss

My son, Stephen, is playing the part
of Jesus in *Godspell*. His best friend,
Evan, is playing Judas, and Judas
must betray Jesus with a kiss.

I am sitting in the third row, waiting.
Judas approaches Jesus and stops.
He can't do it. He can't betray his friend.
Stephen understands. He puts his hands

on either side of Evan's face, just above
the ears, and then he kisses him.
It's all right, he says, I love you.
And the woman next to me asks,

"Do they usually do it like that?"
"No," I answer, "but I like it better
this way. It's not the text, but it's
so beautiful it doesn't matter."

I think this is exactly how Jesus is.
"I love you," he says to us all.
"Do what you have to do and I
will still love you forever."

And he kisses Judas before the guards
come with their sour smell of death.
Did you plan that? I ask Stephen afterwards
or did it just happen? He has never answered.

# In the Museum, Outside the Tomb

From Vermeer, *Woman in Blue Reading a Letter*

At first it is only the light that seems
to change, then the hand holding
the letter moves. I reach toward it.

"Do not touch," says the guard.
I step back startled. I had not known
I was so close. Then I look again,
and slowly, as if by some desperate
ancient spell, her fingers move again.
Her head turns toward me. And my
hands move toward her, my palms
on the silken skin of each cheek.

"Do not touch," says the guard again
somewhere in my dreams. I am gone.

And then Mary, the Magdalen, outside
the tomb on Easter morning, outside the tomb,
her heart beating, her hands reaching like mine
for Jesus, ah my lord, she cries, moving toward
him, toward him. "Do not touch," he says,
his hand raised before her. But she comes on.
She is gone, as I am gone, inside the painting.
"Do not touch," the guard says again. I laugh.
They will never find me. I am there in the shifting
light of the window, as Mary is there in Jesus' arms,
yes, she says, Lord she says, and now she is alone
outside the tomb, her heart beating. "Do not touch,"
Jesus says from somewhere else.

"Do not touch,"
the guard says once again.

# Mary Magdalene

For Clara Dean Abbott on her eleventh birthday

Did you know that July 22 is the Feast Day
for Mary Magdalene, the day we especially
remember her, and you, of course. Like you,
she was—how shall I say it—pretty amazing.

And I thought you might like to know
something about her. She was the first
person to get to the tomb on Sunday
morning, the first to notice Jesus wasn't
there, and the first to actually see him.

There were two others, Peter and John,
who ran to the tomb after Mary told them
it was empty. But they didn't stay. That
was the thing about Mary. She loved Jesus
so much she couldn't bear his absence.

She stood weeping outside the tomb,
and that was why she saw Jesus first.
She just wouldn't leave. She didn't
recognize him, he looked so different,
but when he spoke, she knew the voice.

And she ran to put her arms around him.
She wanted to hug him to death, this
wonderful man she had loved from the
first time she saw him. But he stepped
away and said, "Don't touch me." Think

of that. He was in this new body, one
that you couldn't hug. She was broken
hearted. But Jesus said, "Go tell my brothers,"
and she did, broken heart and all.
"The Lord has risen," she said to them.
She was the first one to see him, the first
to really know, because she loved him
more than anyone else. So you see,

dear Clara, that the women got there first
and they are still getting there first,
still getting the point a little quicker

than the guys. And her Feast Day
is July 22. So, I'll think of her
when I think of you. The two
of you together.

# What I Would Have Told You

I hold them in my heart, these girls, twins,
eighteen, about to graduate from school,
home alone at night, with their brother,
twenty-one, I think. Mother in Nicaragua
or Guatemala, visiting family. My friend,

I want so much to tell you how the storm
came upon them, a giant with plodding feet,
crushing everything in its path, and the girls
frightened by the terrible whip of the
night wind, the crash of thunder—the girls

went to their brother's room, held each other
in his bed while the storm swirled and the
lightning struck and the huge tree toppled
—not on their own bed, as they had feared,
but on the brother's bed where they lay—

killed instantly the paper said. You see
I want to pick up the phone and hear
the sweet silence of you listening to me.
I want to tell you how the girls sought
this one place of safety, and rightly so

and how it offends my sight, this thing—
all of them, of course—Joplin, Tuscaloosa,
St. Louis—all of them day after day—
but these two girls—twins, about to graduate
from school. I name them—Leticia and Celia—

what I really wanted was to tell you the story,
to look at you and ask—what can we say
about this? I wanted you to comfort me,
to tell me it was all right, though it was not
and never could be, never, never.

Perhaps we would have talked about God.
Perhaps I would have cursed or wept
or shouted at the empty sky. Perhaps
you would have touched my hand and told
me of the blue-green veil of mystery.

That's the point, isn't it, my friend. It's not
about the girls or God or justice in the universe.
It's about the flat black emptiness without you.
"Let the days go by," you said in the dusk
out there. I can't. I look for you everywhere.

# Homeless Jesus

He lies there, on a metal bench, feet bare,
the nail holes boring into the very marrow
of our souls. This is not the angry prophet
who threw the money changers from the icy
temple. Oh no, this is Jesus, after what we
did to him. Yes, not they, but we. He is not
sleeping there because some sculptor thought
it smart for his art. God no! He is sleeping there
because we put him there, every day, every
hour, every second.

Look at the size of the holes. A child
was frightened by those holes, someone tells me.
Good. Let the child go home. Let the parents
tell the child what we did to him, what
we still do to him.
                    And you, who read
these words, stop your cars, get out, go sit
with him and talk. Bend down and look
into that sleeping face beneath the hood.
Pour water through his parched lips, bandage
his naked feet. Cover the holes we have made.
Do it now, do it now, do it now, and perhaps
on Easter morning early you'll drive by and see
the bench is bare, the empty cloak crumpled
on the ground.

Meanwhile, in a different town on a back street
in a cardboard box, another homeless Jesus waits.

# Hands

On the ceiling of the Sistine Chapel
Adam waits to be touched into life.
Eve too waiting, hands in a gesture
of prayer, beseeching, adoring, blessing

God for His touch. I also want
the healing of hands, the doctor's
hand on the head of the white-faced dog,
the priest's hand raised in blessing,

the hand of the grandchild pulling
insistently to say— "Play with me!"
I want the fingers of a lover intertwined
with mine. But all around I see

hands striking in anger, turning
knuckle sour, blood under the nails.
Hands run amuck in the desert dirt.
Hands of the drunk driver turning

the wheel too late. Adam's hands
holding the fruit, considering.
Eve's hands praying, waiting,
beseeching.

# At the Christmas Service

*Every valley shall be lifted up, and every mountain*
*And hill be made low, the uneven ground shall become*
*Level, and the rough places a plain.*
                                                    —Isaiah 40:4

Once Handel's notes roused me to joy.
"Every valley," the tenor sang,
and the chorus answered. Back and forth
they rocked through the music, and you could
feel that divine highway slicing through
the ancient hills and dales, turning the very
rivers aside. It was exciting stuff.

Now I only hear the steady grind
of yellow bulldozers, and the crack
and falling of the pines, the slow curves
of hills erased and flat black parking lots
plunked in front of giant stores. Just one
more development.

Let God walk on asphalt, let Him feel the heat
on summer days and the ice in February.
One day, when His judgment comes, we'll
stop laughing, I know, but for today at least
I smile to think of those exalted valleys
and hills made low turning into Los Angeles.

# On Christmas Day, 1927

the poet
    William Carlos Williams
        his family across the sea

drove from Rutherford
    by himself
        to visit the animals at the Bronx Zoo.

In the meadowlands
    he picked up a hitchhiker
        a drifter who wanted

to see New York City
    a man without a dime
        so the poet give him a cigarette

counted out half his money
    and dropped the man
        at the Weehawken ferry.

In the stone-gray shadows
    of the Bronx Zoo's cafeteria
        he ate his Christmas dinner—alone.

# Crèche

From the old French, meaning crib,
sometimes called a manger, from the
old French, meaning to eat, a trough
for the feeding of animals. In any case
a hard place for a child to be born.

In an old house in the front hall
a wooden crèche of simple sticks
and next to it a pile of straw.
Each day during advent family
members contemplate the Christ
child's birthing place, its hardness.

Each day, if they have done something
good, each of them can move some
straw into the crèche to soften the place
where the child will come on Christmas
day. They do not announce their
deeds, but simply follow the dictates
of their consciences, moving the straw,
piece by piece, day by day, as indeed
we must, from the pile to the hard
wood of the crèche. It is, as I
understand, only what Jesus asked.

# Jamie's Prayer

*Dear Lord, bring me through darkness into light. Bring me
through pain into peace. Bring me through death into life. Be
with me wherever I go, and with everyone I love. In Christ's
name I ask it. Amen.*

For Frederick Buechner, its author


When I read the prayer to myself
out loud alone in my room, I felt
the tears come and I knew for the first
time in many months that I would be
all right, that I would find myself again

that the dry ghost of these withering
months would not win after all.

Later, at the meeting, I read the prayer
out loud to the assembled council and said
that it was my favorite prayer, that I had
typed it out to give to anyone who might want
to put it on their bedside table as Jamie had.

I read it slowly with some emotion,
then sat down. At the end of the meeting
no one came up to me. No one wanted
the prayer.

In my room, I took the copies I had made
and cut them into tiny pieces, hundreds
of tiny pieces. Then with both hands full
I hurled the pieces to the ceiling and watched
as they came swirling down, covering
my mending heart with their tiny letters.

# Part Three

## *The Book of Driving and Music*

# Ashes To Go

It is Ash Wednesday. On the sidewalk outside
St. Peter's Episcopal Church downtown
the priest presents the passers-by with ashes.
He makes the sign of the cross on the forehead
of each willing participant. "Ashes to ashes,
dust to dust," he says to their retreating backs.
How handy in this age of convenience.
Soon we will have ashes—online.

I have no time for this nonsense. This is the day
I drive for the Red Cross. I take patients to dialysis.
We call them clients for reasons I do not
understand. My regular number is ten, but today
I have only six. One of them, my friend Ray,
has died, of a massive heart attack, my second death.

Alex, who always helps me, is very sick,
his wife says with a grave face. He has gone
to the doctor. Vicky, the storyteller,
can no longer ride with us. Her wheelchair
will not fit into the van. And Dorothy,
the talker, has decided she no longer needs
to come on Wednesdays. The other six are not much
better. James needs a knee replacement, and they
keep putting him off. Miss Louise has fallen, and her sons
must help her into the car. Miss Dixie is waiting
for her beloved Aunt Aggie to die, and Mr. Berry is too
heavy for me to lift from his wheelchair to the car door.

"We're all dying," Dixie reminds me. "Ashes to ashes,"
says the priest. I feel blessed to know these courageous
souls. They batter against the brittle end of things
forcing their blood through the dark machines
to buy forty-eight more hours.

                    Driving home at noon,
I make the mark of the cross on my own forehead.

# Why Does It Matter Anyway?

The roof on the new house is almost finished
and further down the street the yard of the
remodeled house is solid mud where grass
will one day grow. At dinner we take bets
on when. What did you do today, my wife
asks. I saw the mud from the car, I saw
the new roof from the car. It is the last house
in the development, I say. So what? I think.
Why does it matter, anyway? But here
is something—

In the car for three weeks now, during
my thirty-minute drive to work and my
drive again home, I play the same music,
the soundtrack from the film *The Mission*.
Over and over, the same themes haunt
my soul. I hum them to myself. I whistle
them to myself, I play the whole orchestra
inside my head, haunted by the beauty
of these melodies, haunted by the sound
of Gabriel's oboe. Sometimes I come close
to tears. Is not that better than the mud,
than the almost finished roof?

# This Morning, Driving for the Red Cross

My friend Walter has a new complaint.
You know Walter. He's the one who laughs
at me when I use my "sweet voice" on the phone.

He's the one who's had every imaginable pain,
who could hardly walk to the car from his
front door for weeks this winter, who has
arthritis in his hands, stabbing pains in his
legs, sharp needles in his chest from where
they did the heart surgery. He's a Jehovah's
Witness. This morning he introduced me to
two of his friends. They were lovely, gracious,
They hugged him when he got in the car and
told me to take good care of him.
                                    In the car
he told me his complaint. The doctor had
examined his boobs, he said, and found
a lump. He has to have a mammogram.
James was in the car, in the back seat.
We were the first to find out, he said.
"You want to touch it?" he asked. We
all laughed, we laughed like hell. "You
don't turn me on, Walter," I said. And
we laughed some more.

When Raymond got in the car, in Cornelius,
we didn't talk about it anymore. Raymond
has a '68 Corvette convertible in his garage.
I'm wondering why we're driving him to dialysis.

Walter and I always talk about Jehovah's Witnesses
before James and Raymond get in the car. I'm
different from the other drivers, he says. Yes, I am....

# The Woman Who Went to Jail

She had been drinking shots at her sister's.
Five of them were telling stories about
a friend who had died the night before.

The bottle of vodka lay on the front
seat when the officer stopped her for
speeding. "It's against the law ma'am,"
he said. "But it's not open," she said.
The officer explained the law, which
she did not know, and took her license.
"This license has expired," the officer said.

"Oh officer, I didn't know. I've just moved
here. They never told me." He asked her
to get out of the car, and he administered
a breathalyzer test, which she failed.

"When did you last drink?" he asked her.
"We went to bed at four, and I got up
at seven to get to work," she replied.
"That's not enough time, ma'am,"
the officer informed her, "Oh," she said,
"I didn't know."

He cuffed her and put her in the back
of his car next to the German shepherd.
"I love dogs," she said. "What's his name?"
"Vincent, ma'am," said the officer.

On the way to jail she made friends
with Vincent, and slipped easily out
of the cuffs, with her thin wrists and tiny
fingers. She called her sister on the cell.

"Ma'am," said the officer. "You're not
allowed to do that." "Oh," she said sweetly,
"I didn't know." She put away the cell,
and slipped the cuffs back on.

At the hearing, the officer said she was
the most cooperative person he had
ever arrested. The judge let her off
with a warning.

# The Poem about Driving and Grace

### 1.

At the cleaners he was sure the Korean seamstress
had winked at him. And also the blond girl
at the Human Bean, the coffee-to-go place
he slid into from the cleaners, and then
on the highway he forgot how fast he was
going, because he loved the rollicking piano
strokes of Mozart, and rocking away, he found
he was being followed by a blue light. Sheriff's
deputy.

"What on earth were you thinking?" the young
man asked, and took his license. When he came back,
he shook his head. "This license says you are seventy-two.
I feel like I'm giving my Paw-Paw a ticket. I hate it."

"Yes, sir," the man said, "I appreciate how you feel.
I know you have to do your duty." He smiled at the
lovely young man who hated to give him a ticket.
"I don't know what happened," he said to the officer.
"I'm usually very careful." "Get yourself a lawyer,"
said the officer, "they can knock it down." The two
smiled and shook hands, and off the old man drove,
very slowly, humming the Mozart andante. No more
allegros for a while.

At home he looked up at the sky—
so blue it broke his heart, and the sun glinting on the water.

### 2.

The next day he volunteered for the Red Cross.
When he saw ninety-year old Lucinda Graham,
Miss Lucinda, in her bright green sweater, he told her
how pretty she looked, and he smiled all the way
to the Dialysis Center, where he dropped her off
for treatment and picked up Miss Mary Ann Barringer.
They followed a school bus all the way to her house.

"Aint no use to fret," she laughed, and winked at him.
He did a double take, then laughed himself, kissed
her on the cheek outside her door, and drove home
at twenty miles an hour behind a green tractor. He saw
the rolls of fat on the farmer's neck, and the backs
of the sturdy blue overalls. How strange, he thought,
not to be mad, not to curse the pace of the lone
tractor on the busy road. It just didn't matter.

At home he looked up at the sky—so blue
it broke his heart, and the sun glinting on the water.

# Sitting Alone at the Post Office, Listening to Beethoven's Fifth

Quite simply, it was not over when I arrived
and I could not bear to let it finish without me.

There is this thing about music—that we are graced
once or twice in our lives to hear the actual notes.

Think of Mozart in the film hearing the pure music
rolling the billiard balls across the table, the whole

symphony in his head, every note, and how he loses
it when someone opens the door and speaks.

In the car now, alone, at the post office, I hear
the final movement of the Fifth, and imagine

someone, you perhaps, sitting in the other seat
listening to the notes with me, and how the moment

would be doubled, tripled, transformed into
its own Platonic forms, the essence of musicness

if you like—that pure note which can never
be repeated, only felt in the heart for years

to come in other post offices I might go
to mail a letter to someone, perhaps you,

still imagining how my very soul might have been
shaken from its dull lethargic roots, had you

been there beside me in the car at the post office
when the final movement of the Fifth played that day.

# Pyotr Ilyich and Me

The Brits say he's too bloody blatant
and my brother-in-law that he's
boring and predictable. But somehow

he suits me right now. Oh how I
loved him as a child, all those melodies
one right after another you could hum.

I liked the waiting, the hearing of
the tune in the far distance, the
slight whirr of the violins or the

muffled drums, and how it would
almost vanish, almost die, then
suddenly come back, this time

with the woodwinds and the trumpets
and the full sweep. Here it comes,
Pyotr says, what I promised you all along.

Here I am, driving down the Interstate,
the French have retreated, yes, and the bells
of Moscow peal. The old Russian anthem

bursts forth, the cannons boom. I drive
with one hand, conduct the finale with the other.
The disc comes out, I slip it in, push play,

and wait to do it again, all of it, over again.

## Memorizing Dylan Thomas While Driving for the Red Cross

My first pick up is Robert Reid
who has had three surgeries already
this year and is expecting one more.
*Do not go gentle into that good night.*

*Rage, rage, against. . .* No that is the third
line. *Old age should burn and rage. . .* No *rave—*
God, I can't get it. I drop Mr. Reid at the doctor
and tell him someone else will pick him up.

I must find Mrs. Wiley in Huntersville
before nine o'clock. *Wise men, at their end
know dark is right, but. . .* oh yes, *because
their words had forked no lightning. . .*

OK, Mrs. Wiley, where are you? I can't find
the number of your house. It says here on Mapquest
this is where you live. *Rage, rage, against the dying
of the light.* There is no goddamn 300 on this corner.

Great. I call the office. They can't find it either.
I ask at the Farmer's Market. It might be the old
folks community across the street. Mapquest said
left, this is right. *Wild men, who caught and sang*

*the sun in flight, and learn too late they grieved it.*
Oh I like that one. Mrs. Wiley, where are you?
There are old folks all over sitting on benches outside.
No one knows her. What is her apartment number?

I don't know. *Do not go gentle.* No, I will not go
gentle or otherwise. I call the office. They find out
Mrs. Wiley is in 5B. Ok, I go to 5B. No one answers.
I call her on my cell phone. No one answers. *Rage*

*rage, against the dying of the light.* What if
she's lying inside, dead? Now what do I do?
*Grave men, near death, who see with blinding sight.*
O God, maybe she's gone gentle into that good night.

I call her doctor, who says she's sitting in his waiting
room, calm as can be. Great, and here I am looking
like an idiot. I sit in my car and say the words out loud:
*Old age should burn and rave at close of day.*

*Rage, rage against the dying of the light.*

# Is and Is Not

Because it is and is not the music
because it is and is not the loss
of the very thing that the music is
I do not know how to explain it
I do not know how to bring it back
how for example to make the moment
in Brahms first symphony, the moment
that always brought me to tears, how to
make the moment real again, make
the tears come again, make the music
so real the years do not matter anymore.
Listen! If you can't do it, I have no need
of you. If you can wrap the moment
in wonder once again, take me with you.
By myself I hear only notes.

# Grief

For years he stood stiff as a brass candlestick
while the leaves danced down the street
in their coats of many colors, and the branches

bent before the wind. At the ocean once
he lay awake all night just to hear the waves
crash against the splintered beach, the dark

erasure of time falling back through sand.
Now he knows the cost of such a thing.
In a picture on his shelf, his young daughter

balances her small body on her
haunches, her feet flat on the level sand
as she spells her name in shells before

the tide erases her. Alone in his car
he listens to Mozart, weeps for the perfect
flower of her blossoming and for the dear

friend he drove for weeks on end to her
oncologist, gone now into the white ash
of forgetfulness. And he sees for the first

time the young child reaching through the bars
of her candied crib, fingers spread outward,
listening to the rain on the roof, the thunder—

her parents across the hall, beneath their covers.

# Part Four

## *The Book of Observations*

# A Conversation

For Carol Quillen, President of Davidson College

"Did you hear the President last night?" I ask.
"No," he says.
"She was wonderful," I say. "She asked us to read
promiscuously, to read with passion and joy,
to read everything, to study all sides."
"Did you watch the boys?" he asks.
"What boys?" I ask.
"The basketball team."
"No," I say, "I was listening to the President.
She asked us to live in the gray,
to understand that we are all
many people inside."
"The boys were wonderful," he says.
"They really whipped Mercer."
"She talked about how reading changed her life,
how she read as a child to stem the loneliness,
how she learned from reading what it was like
to be someone else."
"Jack scored 33," he says.
"She asked us to love those who are different,
to understand that truth is always tentative,
ever changing."
"The big guys were tremendous," he says.
"Yes," I say. "She certainly was."

*how she learned from reading
what it was like to be some-
body else.*

# Effluctress

*Today my daughter made up a word... "Effluctress,"*
*she says, are things*
*that can only be seen by 4-year-olds.*

—Scott Owens

Four-year-olds, darling, yes I agree,
completely—it's only the *only*
I have a problem with. Poets,

sweetheart, and lovers, lovers
especially, can see all sorts of things.
So give us a break, my dear,

because we love what you can see
and you'd love what we can see,
too. The other day I was walking

home from church, and all of a
sudden, I said out loud: "Even
the streets are holy." That's right,

out loud, and I looked down
and there in the cracks between
the sections of the sidewalk

I could see I was right. God was
there, in the pieces of the sidewalk.
He told me so. He did, my love,

not in so many words, but you
know how effluctress works.
things don't just come in words.

And then, in the trees over the street
—there was Mary, the mother of God,
in her blue dress with gold embroidered

hem and sleeves. She had very dark
hair and smiled at me as if to say,
"It's all right, don't worry." She stayed

with me for days, kind of floating
along in the trees all over town
just smiling and saying to me

"Don't worry. Let it be." I know,
that's not original, but I couldn't
resist it. And if she's not

effluctress I don't know what is.
I love your rainbow bird outside
the window very much, but this

—this is Mary, the mother of God,
in her blue dress and gold embroidered
hem and sleeves. I'm sure of that.

I know I'm not four anymore
but I sure want to be effluctress
and I just wanted to know, well,

how am I doing?

# Grace

In the blue recycling bucket
    wedged between two bottles
        a luna moth unmoving.

He lifts a bottle off
    sets the moth in his palm,
        such green, such glorious green.

He raises his hand
    to the pink blossoms
        of the mimosa tree.

The moth takes flight
    slowly, tentatively
then surely,

rising
    into the sweet
        June air.

# At the Hummingbird Feeder

It is nearly noon, and we have returned
from a long walk in the woods. We have
seen Quetzels, the kings of the Costa Rican
birds, and we have watched a collared
redstart jump from branch to branch shaking
his pretty red crest only inches away from us.

Now I am alone, writing in my journal
by the hummingbird feeder, watching
them dart and hover, dart and hover,
watching them sitting on the little branches
and then hovering to sip, hovering to sip,
balancing perfectly in the air and throwing
their small heads back after each turn.

The girl comes from the restaurant
to refill their nectar, and while she is
gone, they are distraught. They fly
in circles, alight and fly away. Their
world is empty, forever it seems.

And then she returns. "Oh my darling,"
I say to her in English, "you have
come back." The hummingbirds are
delirious with joy. They sip and sip
and sip until they are full. "Do you know
how much they love you?" I ask. But
she does not understand. "Español,"
she says and smiles. "Oh, how they love
you," I say to her again, and again
she smiles. And the hummingbirds
dance deliriously around the feeder,
taking their fill of the newfound food.
Green and black and blue with yellow
crests, they hover and sip and fly away.
They are happy.

# The Glass Wall

In the prison I visit you. We place
our hands on the glass, palm to palm,
finger to finger as if comparing
the size of our hands. I meet your eye.

I meet your eye and ask my hard question.
Why did you do it? Why bolt from the minimum
security unit where we shared the freedom
of Saturday visits at my home
with my wife, my three sons. You made rockets
out of wood for them and for me you crafted
pictures from the stone and dirt of the prison
yard where we sat at outdoor tables
and wrought words over bad coffee. They found
you in a girl's apartment in Atlanta
and carried you to this place where the glass
wall separates us. But that isn't the issue
and we both know it. Sweet Jesus, why
didn't you tell me why you were here
to begin with? You know I found the box
while you were gone with the trial transcript
and the bloody, stupid tale of how you
bludgeoned the poor disabled boy to death,
then buried him in the woods by the river
and drove off with the other men to Florida.

I do not love lightly, I tell you. Once I do
it is forever, no matter what. Do you
know that? I do now, you say. Don't forget,
I whisper, then I knock on the glass,
look you in the eye, turn and walk away
through three sets of bars that open and close
behind me, three sets of bars that clang
and slide, clang and slide until I am alone
in the open air and once more free.

# Prince Charming Revisited

In the fairy tales why is it
always the woman who gets
saved at the end by the handsome
prince? This really pisses me off.

Snow White eats the apple, lies
there like death. And Sleeping Beauty?
What was it—a thorn, a needle?
I can't remember. Even Cinderella

in her own way, rescued from
the bloody stepsisters by the prince.
You get the point. And me, dumb
old me, I was thinking about today,

how it's really the men who need
rescuing, all of us sleeping somewhere,
too tired to rise, waiting for the woman
to somehow kiss us into life

into something more than beer
swilling gas guzzlers driving down
the choking highways to jobs
we really hate. The rescuing princess.

Why not? Diana back from the dead,
Kate who makes her man into a real
prince at last. I don't know. Rescue me,
we cry at the bottom of the well,

but nobody, not even the moon,
can hear our cries.

# Poem in Two Voices

### 1.

You know how the houses of the old smell?
Like some animal's been closed up there
for twenty years. My grandma sits on the
cracked leather sofa, her skirt hiked over
her bony knees. She watches *General
Hospital.* I try to speak, but everyone
knows you can't talk to the old. They don't know
anything. They think a blackberry's
a piece of fruit (ha! ha!). Grandma sometimes
plays Frank Sinatra on her old 33
record player, or even Tony Bennett
who's still alive stuffed with Botox or some
other stuff.
                    "I don't own anything
that has initials," she laughs. "CD,
DVD, VCR, SOB." "What's that,
Grandma?" I ask. She smiles. "I still write
letters by hand," she tells me. "It feels
more personal." Once, when she was young,
she took a boat across the ocean. Six days
with no mail, no phone, no nothing. "It was
heavenly," she says. My cell phone rings.
"I got to go," I say. "You see?" she says,
"That's what I mean."


### 2.

He's a nice boy. He's got his mother's eyes
though I don't tell him that. Once a week
he saunters in the door with his baggy shorts
and his Nike basketball shoes. He slouches
in the easy chair. I sit on the couch. Take off
your hat, Jerome, I say. We talk about
cell phones and iPods and blogs. "You should pay
your bills online, Grandma," he says, "and if
you want I'll sell some of this old stuff on eBay."

He likes everything spanking new. He even
dates on eHarmony, where he'll find
the perfect match.
                    I liked the older pace
of things much better. It scares me how they
go on. Everybody knows everything
right away. All this dinging and banging
and clanging and beeping and driving down
the road talking away. Wasn't the silence
better and those moments nobody could
find you? Still, he's a nice boy. He kisses
me when he leaves and tells me he'll be back.
He always comes.

# Small Town Blues

When we first moved here fifty years ago
the traffic was so light, the dog could lie down
in the middle of Main St. and lick the white line.
Or he could saunter down the street unaccompanied
to the art gallery my wife owned and greet the customers.

Now there are only cars and condominiums,
thousands and thousands come from God knows where
and doing God knows what. A certain charm still exists
if you can find a parking place, which is doubtful, and then
you have to walk to the end of the block to cross
because jaywalkers will be prosecuted. Good grief.

I used to walk from my house to school in five minutes
cutting between the church and the science building
then strolling with joy down the long shady walk
to my third-floor office. Now I roll my stroller
into CVS Drugs and hustle to the back to use the restroom.

Listen. This morning I thought to send a book of mine
to a friend and I couldn't find its name in my mind.
Parking places be damned. Maybe there's something
else I should be thinking about. Something precious.

# The Crazy Man Talks to the Dogs

"The moon shines bright in the hard
silence of the shifting dark," he says
to the small flat-nosed Pekingese.

"In the midnight mass of the Milky Way
the brightest stars are blue," he whispers
to the angular Great Dane.

He likes to walk at night. He likes
the scarved and coated carriers
of the dogs. He likes the cold.

His glittering eyes roam the tops
of the turning trees. "The deer
won't run if you stand very still,"

he says to the happy retriever,
golden under the streetlight
in the tumbling hours.

"It's all a mistake," he mouths
to the wide-chested Boxer,
who slobbers with excitement.

"There is no such thing as hell,"
he cries to the testy terrier,
"Only the brown lawn of forgotten spring."

The owners know nothing. They see
only a strange man who
walks by every night.

It is odd, they say to themselves,
that he never speaks.
But he seems perfectly harmless.

# The Crazy Man Visits the Zoo

"On yellow lined sheets my mother
wrote poems," he says to the spotted
leopard, who blinks twice with her dark

round eyes, "When I came in the room
she put them away, and held me
against her breast so I couldn't breathe."

DON'T FEED THE ANIMALS, the sign says,
so he flips a peanut to the baboon, who
barks like a maddened dog. The crazy

man barks, too. They stare at each other
in delight. "I love your long fingers,"
he says, looking at his own twisted hands.

"I was handsome once, but I don't
remember when. Now my beard
smells of last night's leavings."

"The feathered god makes waves
in the sky," he says to the peacock.
"Save me with your anguished cry."

The reptile house is damp and dark.
"The underside of God," says
the crazy man. "Beware the parting

of the grass, and the lemon smell
of the late summer rain. Take shelter,"
he says to the antelopes across the way.

He raises his eyes high to the circling
hawk, who bends to the shimmering pool
and dives. The keepers cry for solace
and the crazy man laughs his laugh.
The hyena answers, and the red bird
lights on his shoulder. The crazy man

kisses the bird.

# The Man Who Fought with His Computer

He knew it would one day come to this—
the computers taking over as they did
in the old science fiction movies, editing
his punctuation, changing lower case
to capitals, and suggesting even new words.

One day the computer overreached. Now
it was war. He had a signed a student letter
Dr. A, short for Dr. Abbott, informal, friendly—
but the computer had insisted he change it
to "drab." "Drab" indeed. He was not drab,

not in the least. Some of the computer's
ideas were passable, even funny. Calling his
nephew Stu "stud." Or his poet friend Valentina
Gnup "gnu" or even "gun." His favorite was
"grandpa renting" which the computer derived

from "grandparenting." Yes, the grandchildren
did, on some level, rent their grandpa, and to suggest
his grandpa name, Babbo, be changed to "baboon"
was only reasonable from a computer point of view.
But to call his dog "Junie" a "Junkie" was simply

an insult, as was the idea that Frederick Buechner
was a butcher. Butcher indeed, Mr. Computer,
it is you who butchers the English language,
putting a turban on my friend Turhan's head
and reducing Montaigne to a montage.

Ah well, you are not so smart after all, you
with your oh so clever ideas like reducing
St. Louis to "stylus" or MWF to MIFF or MUFF.
But I must admit that calling Professor Emily
Seelbinder "spellbinder" shows true imagination.

So see if you can do better than "drab."

# The Same Woman

On Vermeer's *A Lady Writing* and *Woman with a Pearl Necklace*

The same model
the same lemon
yellow jacket

ermine bordered.
I like to think
she is the same

woman, the letter
writer looking
at us with that

soft, cryptic smile
as if she is
pleased with herself

the same way she
is in the other,
holding that necklace

up toward the window
the mirror
looking at herself

the same way she
is looking at us
as if to say I know

I am lovely
and I know
I'm supposed to be

modest, but
goodness I am
a beautiful creature.

# The White Dress

At Emily Dickinson's house, Amherst

Going up the stairs in your house
going up the stairs and turning
going up the stairs and seeing
the white dress there
in the front window
and turning then into
your room and seeing the small
bed and the bureau
and a table and chair
the room white the furnishings
spare, and then suddenly
you appear yourself
your red hair—that's what seizes me—
the red hair and the smile
and the impish, roguish
sense of humor and the white
dress, you are wearing the white
dress, and smiling, as if to say,
all these years you have got me wrong—
you have got me wrong, you stupid,
plodding pedants. Stop bowing
and think of me now with my
incandescent smile and my rueful
laugh at life's absurdities. Here I am
in my white dress at the top
of the stairs. That's as far as I will go.

# In the Coffee House

With apologies to Billy Collins

The Davidson Elementary School is closed.
The IB Middle School is closed, Davidson
Day School is closed, the Community School
of the Arts and Woodlawn School and the Cannon
School are all closed. Even the United Methodist
and the Davidson College Presbyterian Church
Preschools are closed, and surely the Lakeside
Montessori and the Children's Schoolhouse
are also closed.
              The coffee house is empty.
The college students with their energetic
laptops and their earpieces have gone home,
and the mothers who talk in groups of two
and three, the mothers who have discussed
with such animation all spring the good
teachers and the bad, the politics of private
vs. public—the mothers are all home
scrambling eggs for breakfast, begging
their boys to rise and shine, combing
the hair of their lovely daughters.

Upstairs, a solitary poet sits . . . The silence excites
him. He will not be distracted today. He will
not have to put up with all the dialogue, the banter,
the silly giggles and the whispers. Today he will
write his masterpiece, alone, undisturbed.

He thinks about the cell phone talkers,
who seem to feel they are invisible
—how they talk about everything—
politics and socialtics and love affairs,
talking to the air as if no one else were there.
They, too, are gone. Thank God. It is quiet.
Church committees are the worst. They talk
and talk and talk—blah, blah, blah. Boring gossip
about budgets and books and boxes. And those
church ladies, they're not even . . . he stops himself.

He waits for inspiration. Nothing comes. And then
he remembers the class he took. Yes, exercises, warm
up. Use your words, the teacher said. Ah yes, he thinks,
the alphabet. Twenty-six words, each one a new letter,
from A to Z. Oh good. Always Be Cheerful. Good.
Don't Ever Frown. Get Heavily Into Justice, Kindness, Love,
Mercy. Never Omit Prayer. My God, what is this, he asks?
A Sunday School Bulletin? Question Rowdy Seekers.
Trample Under Vipers. White Xmas Your Zenith.

That's the stupidest poem he's ever seen.

Quiet. Quiet. Dead quiet. Damn, he thinks,
where the hell are all the women?

# Two Friends

My two friends are having lunch.
I am not invited. I think about this
for a long time. Perhaps they wish

to talk about me, to talk about
things they do not wish me
to hear. They wish privacy

so that they can share
with one another words
and images that would seem

uncomfortable if I were there.
I do not know this. It may not
be true at all. Perhaps they simply

wish to have girl talk, to talk
about clothes or their bodies
or the state of their grown

or nearly grown children.
They are tired, tired from
the challenges of work,

of single parenting, or preparing
for the always frantic rumble
of the Christmas season, now

no longer even Christmas.
Happy holidays we say
careful to offend no one.

They have their stresses,
and in their hearts there is
nothing they could share
with me that I would understand.
I know nothing. They are
having lunch and sharing

their laughter across the table
with a small glass of white wine.
I stay at home reading, waiting

for the phone to ring.

# The Word in the Window

Cold outside. Windows frosted.
Inside hot coffee steaming. I sit
by the window reading. At the table
in front of me, two lovers.

I can only see their backs, but I know.
I can tell by the comfort of their hands
and the way their necks arch toward
each other like silent swans.

The girl turns to the window
and draws a heart on the damp glass.
In the pane below, she draws
a second heart. She turns to me

and smiles. The words in my book fall
like shadows into the white margins.

# Part Five

## *The Book of Departures*

# Moving Sale

I am parked at the top of the hill.
The cars stretch all the way to the bottom.
They don't know me, these strangers
who burst from the door of our home
carrying what they can haul away
in their white pickup trucks, their black vans.

A woman in purple shorts waits to get in.
I stand in the yard under the deodara cedar
and watch the lamps and tables glide
into the spring morning. The azaleas
are almost gone, brown at the edges.
Someone has even bought the doormat.

I walk around the back, and hear the small
waterfall empty into the pond. I climb
the stairs to the deck and into the dining
room where the gold chandelier still glows.
My friends stand in line and hold their purchases
up to me. Tell me the story of this one,

a neighbor asks, holding the glass elephant
my patient from dialysis gave me. Another
has a tiger, and the two Kabuki actors I bought
in Cambridge fifty years ago stride out the door
in someone's arms. Upstairs, a beautiful cherry
bureau stands in the empty bedroom. No one

has bought it. Not for sale, I scrawl on a scrap,
and take the small brown bird with metal feet
from a nearby shelf where twenty copies of my
first book wait to be shoveled off to Habitat
or to the trash. The Degas dancers still hang
on the wall of the guest bedroom downstairs.
At the end of the day I will come back for them.
It's hard to breathe the air of so much history.
Our life parades on down the hall and out the door.
A pickup truck backs up into the yard. The double
bed is loaded in the back. The wheels spin and
the truck leaves angry ruts in the soft spring grass.

# The Departures

After the waving, after the goodbyes,
after the car had wound down the drive
and disappeared, I thought about what
it carried—my son, my daughter-in-law
and three grandchildren bearing certain
marks, marks of peace, of beauty, of hope.

All day they would drive west, carrying
not only their precious selves but the last
of the pieces from our old house, a transfer
as it were from our lives to theirs.

The Nordfeldt oil painting of The Last Supper,
which hung over the couch in our living room
for twenty-four years, and before that
in the other house, somewhere—I can't
picture it—those twelve looking past Jesus
into the vacant space that is our lives, looking
at us as if to say—you wouldn't have done
any better.
                    And my granddaughter, sixteen,
with the two Degas prints I bought in Cambridge
and hung in our first apartment, pencil and chalk
on green paper, the ballerinas as lovely as their
new owner, ready to grace whatever stage she chooses.

And the silver tea service, tray and all, with my
grandmother's initials, which my grandfather kept
for years after my grandmother's death in New York
City, and gave to me because my wife and I would
serve tea to the students on the college campus.
It should have gone to my sister, but there was no
place to show it in her small apartment in the Bronx.
How the set, polished bright, glowed on the sideboard
in our dining rooms for forty-eight years. And how it will
continue to glow on the same sideboard, now
in their dining room in St. Louis.

Time switches gears.
We carry the memory of our grandparents, mothers, fathers, aunts, and uncles in their beds and chairs, in the objects they loved. Their faces call us out of ornate, silver frames and boxes with vaguely remembered initials.

These girls were my grandfather's, Clara will say to her friends. He bought them when he was in graduate school. I see them looking down at her and bowing shyly.
They will keep watch over her at night, and smile at her each morning.

# In the Retirement Home: Eva

The carpet on the first floor is blue
the carpet on the second floor is green
the carpet on the third floor is red
the carpet in the lobby on the first floor
is also green, which sometimes confuses me.

I live on the blue floor, but sometimes
I walk the red floor for exercise. I read
the names on the doors and examine
the doodads. There are glass porpoises
and vases with flowers. I touch them

to see if they are real. Sometimes I
forget my whole name. Sometimes
I walk and walk and my mind wanders
to the sea, where I lived as a girl.
They want to put me in health care.

They say I am too much trouble,
that I disturb the others with my talk.
The lady at the end of my hall is after me.
On the green floor you can walk outside
and sit in the sun. The nurses tell me

I will catch cold, but I don't think so.
They watch me. They all watch me.
They are waiting for me to do something
strange so they can put me in health care.
I am nice to everyone. I talk to them

in the halls as I pass by and in the dining
room I spoon my food with care and speak
nicely to the ladies at my table. I smile
and smile. They nod their heads and watch.
Tomorrow, I say, my son will come to visit.

# In the Retirement Home: Patrick

The waiter calls me Mr. Wheeler.
"Call me Patrick," I say, but he likes
Mr. Wheeler. They are all nice to me
here in this piece of starched heaven,

these linen tablecloths and smiles
and gestures of perfect amiability.
I am safe here. They see to my
every need. The ladies speak with

gentle tones of the old South.
At the lectures I sit in the third row.
My children telephone on Sunday.
They do not come to visit. They are

happy I am here. My son called once
to thank me for choosing this house
of zinnias and marigolds. The weather
is fine. I walk on the leafy lanes.

The grandchildren are busy, they
take trips assigned by school. They
write cards with pictures of hearts.
I love you, they say. They travel

to South America and Europe,
and send pictures to my computer.
Yesterday we went on a steamboat
ride around the local lake.

I am happy here.

# In the Retirement Home: the Widows

From T.S. Elliot's "The Hollow Men"

We are the widows.
Leaning together at the table of eight
we whisper of past transgressions
we whisper of happier times.
At the tables of four
the matched couples snicker
smartly between bites.
They glance at us furtively.

We are the widows
We waver like the grass in winter
blown sideways
by the strong wind.
We bend and bend.
We watch Masterpiece Theatre
and retire early.

The wives eye us.
The husbands are frail
and the wives watch the husbands
spill on their new ties,
the wives watch the husbands
trip over their words with their
loosening mouths.

Soon they will be like us. We will
welcome them to our tables.
We will whisper of past transgressions
and they will be thankful.
We will take them to the puzzle rooms
and give them the corner pieces
to put in.
We will smile and whisper
of happier times.

# A Day with the Doctors

They call me Herbert. Well, Herbert,
how are you, they ask. And I think
if I were fine I wouldn't be here.
But I say fine. This morning, early,
I see my primary care physician.
He says I need to see an orthopedist.
They make me an appointment for noon.
At nine-thirty my dentist calls. "Herbert.
we have a cancellation." Good, I think,
I'll get that over with. So I take my required
anti-biotics and get my teeth cleaned.
At noon the orthopedist says I need an MRI.
He doesn't notice my shiny white teeth.
The MRI is for 2:30. They squash me into
the long tube and push my arm up next to my head.
In the tunnel I sing songs to myself, I make up
stories, and try to imagine why it makes the loud
banging noise. Thirty minutes for each arm.
In three days the orthopedist will tell me
how bad it is. Just an ordinary day, another
damned ordinary day. Dermatologist tomorrow.

# No Time to Make Desserts

My doctors are clustered together
as if to make my visits easier, as if
they somehow sought my happiness
in these strange waning days when
I am still, at least, parking in those
wonderfully convenient handicapped
spaces. But I digress.

My oncologist, the most important,
of course, is in the middle of the complex
with the heart doctor, what do you call him,
ah the cardiologist, on the right, as you drive in,
and further on the right in the next building
the urologist, a name that's easy to remember
somehow, and then, on the left, the vein doctor,
whom I happen to know because his wife
sings beautifully in our church, and then,

across the highway, maybe four or five blocks,
the other doctors, virtually next to each other—
ophthalmologist, ear-nose-throat, and finally
my what-do-you-call-it—what do you call it?
Ah, primary care—right? The one who always
sends you to one of the others.

All huddled together. God, how convenient.
It's almost a relief to have to drive twenty miles
to my wound doctor, whom I didn't know
existed until sent there by Primary Care.

Busy day, as my wife, likes to say,
no time to make dessert, with two s's.

# Something to Be Done

To have started something at once
the day before the day before yesterday
when the doctor said non-small-cell
lung cancer, stage 3A, three much better
than four and A than B. All a matter
of statistics. You do what they tell you
and take your chances. You stay happy,
eager to fight even as the weight goes down
and the color drains, and the pants
drag loose about the waist and the
shoulders of the jackets slide off
down the arms. Listen, who cares?
What matters is the surge of the soul
down the steps to the water. What
matters is the color of the sky, as the sun
sinks southwestern into the blue lake
and it is still possible for something
to be done. Better than watching TV
in the living room hooked up to the spiraling
green cord of oxygen. What matters
is what can be done for the fours
and fives.

# The Man Who Lived between Moments

spooned the green pea soup into his mouth
with great deliberation. He wore his bib now, careful
not to spill on his new striped tie. The dining

room at the retirement home was friendly.
Talk of recent events, of ailments and illnesses
floated like colored balloons through the dry

night air. God was not mentioned, nor the scenes
early in Mark's Gospel where Jesus hurried
from town to town, the disciples trailing after

wondering who this man was, trying
so hard to understand what was happening
and why they had left their homes, their nets

to follow him. The man had read these scenes
years ago with a friend. He could remember
the sound of her voice, the way the words

shone with light, the way even the road
the disciples walked ground into his
consciousness like sand blowing.

After supper, he went back to his room
and took his Bible down from the shelf.
He read the scenes, but they were not the same.

# Suppose

Suppose you
have been away for a very
long time

and perhaps you
have been in prison or if that
is too much

just suppose
you have been very sick
and the view

from the hospital
room includes nothing but the
back wall

of another wing
and now you come home
and it is October

very late October
when the leaves have just
reached their

fullness
yes, October in the south
and you have

forgotten
no that is entirely wrong
because you

do not forget
anything. I don't know.
The point is

you have not
seen the beauty of this
lovely place

for a very
long time and you suddenly
are given

three days
let us say to walk around
your town

to walk through
the cemetery while the
maples flame

and the oaks
are yellow gold and the
graves

of your old
friends and teachers lie
like invitations

in the still
green grass telling you
of time before

and you walk
on the campus and stand before
the pistache

with its
thin pointed burgundy
leaves

and you see
the way it glows red and orange
while the trees

behind are
still green like a guardian
hovering

and suppose
you walk down your very own
street

and see the house
and the bright orange maple
across the way

in the empty
lot the builders can't use
and you watch

the way the
sun glances off the trunks
with that

sidelong glance
of almost not yet winter
and you

walk in
the door and you touch
the pictures

of your
grown children and their
children

and think
of the children they will have
one day

when you
are gone and the house
and the pictures

too will be
gone and you walk out again
later and see

the crescent moon
sharp against the clear black
night

and you
and the dog walk down the
familiar street

which now
shines with strangeness with
the unearthly

light of
eternity itself and you weep
for this day

and the two
others you have been given
to come back

before you
are gone again into whatever
place they send you.

Suppose all
this my friend and give thanks
and touch

the petal
before it falls to the ground.
You cannot bring it

back.

# The Long Afternoon

All through the long afternoon
the wind moved in the branches.
I had lived in the city and had seen
only the dust from the tires,
the diesel gas from the gray brown
buses with their leaden burdens.

Here it was different. Here on the grass
we had found by chance, walking
away, just away from everything
and then, a clearing and green
grass and the wind moving
like silver over the water
and in the branches, too. Yes,

all through the long afternoon
the wind moved and we were silent
in awe of the day and the leaves
yellow and red and orange,
which floated slowly down
into our waiting hands.
                              Later
I found these leaves in a book
where you had put them for
safe keeping, a book you knew
I would take down and read
some distant starry night.

# Part Six

*The Book of These New Days*

# These New Days

These new days are like snow in November—
beautiful and white and troubling.
The left foot leaves a small and crooked track.
The right drags slightly over uneven
ground. Each uncertain step perhaps the last.

What do I know now? Less it seems than ever
before. The wisdom of age is nonsense.
Treachery and forgetfulness. Who cares?
The next generation and the next come
hammering at the door. It is their turn.

They are hungry. They cry for entrance.
What can I say? Go take your dirty words
elsewhere? Surely not. Come to my table
and I will limp to you with sharp pencils.
While you write, I will look out the window

and watch the snow, white and troubling.

# Half Moon

Half moon high in the night sky
sliding upward from the cover
of trees. I stand on the deck

and look, then close the door
and go to bed. No more of this.
No more music, no more pounding

the beat of the old songs
on the steering wheel,
no more singing the remembered

words. No more plucking
of the red leaves, no more
silence before the mystery

of elusive grace caught
in the winnowing air.
I will sleep now, for a long

time perhaps and rise
once more to a day's work.
I will start now, to see

what artifact can be made
from the slim remains
of reconstructed time.

# Object Lesson

It is Sunday. I am picking up sticks
in my yard. I place them on the ashes
of the old fire. I crumple paper
and light it. Then I gather more sticks.

On Mondays we would read together,
poetry perhaps, or passages
from the Gospels. Sometimes I would recite
poems to you that I had learned by heart.

It is Tuesday and I am balancing
my checkbook. I will package the retainer
my grandson left in the downstairs bathroom
and carry it to the post office.

On Wednesday evenings I would often give
lectures at the local churches. On the drive
home I would telephone you and tell you
about the people and how their faces shone.

It is Thursday and I am driving
for the Red Cross, carrying patients
to dialysis and to the doctor.
I love the quiet courage in their hearts.

On Fridays we would take the dogs for walks.
Sometimes our paths would cross and we would talk
together and share the stirrings of our souls
under the branches of the bending trees.

It is Saturday. There are guests in the house.
I cook steaks on the grill, and afterwards
we play cards. There is much laughter.
I forget to look for the full moon.

# Next of Kin

For whom is the poem
written?

For the beloved
of course

but if the beloved
is not,

then for the next
of kin

which is like water
on the tray

after the ice has
melted.

# October

The tea olive is
out again

I stagger down the
stone steps

late afternoon
the scent

wild as sweet
honey

my heart is
broken

# Of What Do I Speak

*Old Men Should Be Explorers*
—T.S. Eliot

This morning I search for worms
in the compost and carry them
wriggling splendidly in the plastic
cup to the grandchildren. The girls
cast their lines. Fishes rise.

*A long time ago we walked on the beach.*
*We talked about God and the mystery*
*of death.*

This afternoon in the boat I pull
the girls around and around
over the rising wake. They scream
with delight and ask to go again.
At five we buy ice cream.

*I feared nothing then. I recited poems*
*to strangers and wrote, late into*
*the night.*

Tonight I cook cheeseburgers
on the grill and play games
with the girls. When they win
they beg to play again. It is late
when they go to bed.

*At the end, I walked alone*
*on the beach and scattered my memories*
*along the tumbling dunes.*

# Quite the Opposite

of life, that is, these odd days edging
into the ether world. The having lived,
the having had—I know all that.
"You've had a good life," they say.

But stay, put yourself here. Leer
if you will at this stupid old man
who begs for one more bite, and gets
instead these odd days, as I say,

these doddering edgings into sleep
into the wax figures of dreams
and the phone ringing, shocking
him back. "Hello," he says

to some damned solicitor selling
vitamins or hearing aids or some
stupid prosthesis, or some frantic
pollster wanting his opinion on

world affairs about which he knows
nothing, just dozing here waiting
for the splendid moment, the light,
the sound of stars smashing,

rainbows parting under the curved
waves of the pounding surf. Sleeping
again, a pool of water on the page
of his open book, the pencil on the floor.

# The Man Who Loved Trees

kept his distance this year as if he knew,
as if the dark possibility which haunted
his inner mind could only be kept at bay
by stark denial, a looking the other way.

And then one day, he forgot, and found
himself there at the very spot, and when
he finally brought his eyes up from the brick
walk to the tree itself, he knew he was right.

She was ordinary now, leaves still intact
but mustard brown and dry, dry as the dust
which had choked the air that fall, dry as his
own heart, which had slowed to a walk.

If you don't wake her, he thought, the muse
goes back to sleep, malnourished, the roots die.

# The Man Who Is Sorry

wishes he had done better, wishes he had
stopped by the roadside to help the black man
stranded with a flat tire, wishes he had sat
by his dying father's bedside.

Too bad, he says to the sky. Too bad, he says
to the tree whose name he does not know.
Too bad he says to the flowers and the birds
and the insects whose names he does not know.

Is the wisdom of age a farce? At the art
gallery the pictures look alike. He cannot
think of what to say. "That one is nice."
Sweet Jesus, not much different from dead.

He wants to live, this man who is sorry,
wants to know something, brilliantly and finally.

# The Nameless

The African American man with glasses
who carves the tenderloin on Sunday mornings
at the retirement home, the man who played
baseball once with my youngest son.

The British singer, one of many who was
knighted, who wrote a song in memory of
Marilyn Monroe, then performed it with different
words at the funeral of Princess Diana.

The judge from Little Rock whose daughter
played with Chelsea Clinton growing up,
who came to our house for Thanksgiving
while a student at Davidson College.

The former English major with bright red
lipstick, now an Episcopal priest, who
sat in the third seat in the front row
in three different literature classes.

How they drift in and out of namelessness,
caught for a moment in a bright flash
of light, then gone again for months
at a time drifting with other forgotten

down the green streams of the lost.

# Temporarily Out of Order

I am talking to a friend about singers.
"Who is your favorite?" he asks.
I am stumped. The silence snaps the branch
of my attention. "Yellow Brick Road,"
I think, and the one about his father.
"Your Song," and the one for Princess Di
originally about Marilyn Monroe.

"George," I think, but that is wrong.

Another conversation. "When you were
in Italy, did you visit any wineries?"
"Yes," I say. "Which one?" Another silence.
Near Montalcino. Very famous. Brunello da
Montalcino. We ate lunch there, and drank
that gorgeous wine.

In bed, at night, I recite poems to myself
in the dark. I say them over and over
until each word is right. Then I can sleep.

# The Man Who Reads the Newspaper

shifts in his tired chair and scratches beneath
his left shoulder. The news is always bad.
Three boys have killed a llama and cut its
body into pieces "just for the fun of it."

The stock market is down and the rising dollar
makes trade more difficult. It is Friday
and the sudoku is especially hard.
He turns to the sports section for solace

but his favorite team has lost again and
his horoscope warns him to be careful.
It is only a three-star day. Clouds are
forming to the west. It will surely rain.

He loved once, this man, and felt even
in his bones the glint of the wave and the
sharp thrust of the heron's beak as he stabbed
at the silver fish. The moon smiled silently

at his ready eye and his tongue made music
from the falling leaves and the early dust
of snow. Now he stares out the window
and wonders how he will spend the day.

It will be too cold to walk. He will read
his biography and look up the unknown
words on his smart phone, the lost places
of the heart dim in the haze of another dawn.

# Part Seven

## *The Book of the Last*

# What the Heart Knows

The dark art of the sea at night
white curl of waves seeking
the smooth sand—moon above
enveloping all with its silver light,
shimmering curtain calling you
to the window or perhaps
to walk barefoot on the beach.

What the heart knows, the heart
knows. The heart makes the scene,
the heart takes the wave, the sea,
the moon, creates the magic
of the night remembered. Too
bad if you missed it. It may not
come again, ever.

# Waiting

In the morning the man
sits at his desk

he reads a multitude of
messages

but nowhere are the words
for which he is. . .

In the afternoon he dozes
in the green chair

and listens for the roll
of curling waves

a sound for which
he is. . .

Late at night he steps out
from his lighted house

and sees the full moon
looming

over the dark roof top
but it is not

the light for which
he is. . .

# Do Not Forget This

Each morning, when you awake
    kneel down and place your forehead
        on the floor, the ground, the carpet,

wherever you are. Give thanks
    for the life of your wife
        give thanks for your sons

Speak their names
    one at a time, each morning.
        Do not ask for anything

Do not hope.
    That for which you hope
        will not occur.

Be thankful for the gift of life
    and the small birds who drink
        from the pool outside your window.

Then rise and start the day.

# Unfinished Sentence

Yesterday the precise sky
   shattered our senses
      the pure blue stunned
      our hearts

today the gray comes
   again, an old dog
      snoring under the dining
      room table like an

unfinished sentence ending
   in the word
      "but"

# On the Morning After

the words vanished
tumbling it seems letter
by letter into the green sea

the "l's" and "m's" sinking
into the primeval darkness
even divers do not reach

the newspaper boxes
startlingly empty
the mouths of the reporters

making soundless motions
the computer screen
a dazzling tweetless blue

on that morning after
the sun still shone
in the innocent sky

the heron still stood
one-legged on the
weathered dock

and on a bare branch
of the highest pine
the hummingbird kept watch.

# Poem in the Key of A

On a day in May
late afternoon
I lay on a grassy bank

The dogs waded
into the shimmering lake
and drank deep

They were at peace
and I too was at peace
on the grassy bank

I look up at the sky
at the trees quivering slightly
in the May breeze

at the gold of the sun
darting between the leaves
and then I laugh

and I laugh again
louder this time.
And shout, "I have wasted my life!"

The trees laugh
the lovely lake laughs
the dogs laugh

even the grassy bank laughs
here in the late afternoon
on this day in May.

# Second Spring

I sit on the grass
in the small park behind
the red brick library.

The dogwoods
are in full bloom
and the red azaleas just

coming round the corner
to their richness.
The Japanese tulip

waves from higher ground.
I read "Fern Hill"
out loud to myself

and the moment opens like a gift.
There are no words for this—
only the stunned silence

of here and now, my soul
awake to this second spring.

# Rain

I am walking with the dog
in the rain. It is the first
day of school, and I am passed
by two yellow school buses.

The dog squats in the wet grass
and the children laugh. I see
their glee through the misty
windows. I am drenched through

and through, the dog is soaked
and the children must wonder
at the sight of this older man
his hair flattened by the rain

walking along the roadside
with his white-faced friend.
I have never been so happy.
I give thanks for the rain

which soaks the roots of the trees
and gives life again to the small
plants and the nameless purple
wildflowers the mowers have missed.

I rejoice in this wetness, this glorious
shining wetness for which we have
prayed for two years. When we get
home I will towel the dog, and she

will tremble with joy at the touch
of the dry, soft cloth on her back.
In the shower I will let the water
play upon my face and hair

and listen to the rain dancing on the roof.

# Snow in the City

They descend from the second-floor stoop.
The dog's paws make the first prints

of the morning. Cars sleep, the eyes
of their windshields lidded white.

The dog walks freely, no restraint today,
sniffing her way around the corner to the

glowing bakery. They breathe in the ecstasy
of fresh-made rolls. The dog waits outside

while the man talks to the white hatted
baker. No school today, no laughing

children for her to lick. She lies down
in the doorway. The man comes out

holding in his hand the white bag
of muffins. He reaches in, breaks off

a piece. "Sit," he says, and the dog sits.
"Eat," he says, and the dog eats.

# That Without Which

The moment itself not being but coming into
or having been the moment itself that which
we wait for live for then like the five o'clock
winter sun fading into a rustle, a blowing
of the window curtains door to the balcony
open to the wind the walking on the beach
the stars the ringing of the communion bell
and the knowledge priceless that this might
have never been could never be but was
and is the moment which gives to all life
the aura of the mysterious, the sacred,
blessed and consecrated by the heart under
another name not known but felt how could
we live otherwise

# After the Ringing

of the last bell
he kneels
on the cold stone

and takes the cup
and drinks from it.
"Ah well," he thinks,

"this is what it will
be like from now on.
I will hold out

my hand to the homeless
man who begs
at the highway's end.

I will drive the needy
to their white-coated doctors
and listen to their tales.

I will send cards
to my friends
on their birthdays.

I will walk in the early
evening and watch
the moon rise

in the east
as the pink sky blends
with the darkening blue
in the dying west.
The black branches
will fork out

into the coming night."

# The Last

The last walk, he thinks, the last stroll
down the wooded path with the dog
sniffing in the cool morning air.

The last knock on the red door.

The last subway ride—New York,
London, Paris. The ungovernable
steps. The violins at the Louvre.

The last sigh under the stone stairs.

Better not to know. Tomorrow
or ten years. Better to receive
each morning as a wrapped gift.

The last glimpse of the crescent moon at midnight.

The last swim in the smooth lake,
the last flash of the sun
as it sinks into the sea.

The last wave reaching high and sliding back.

The last poem, the last linking
of lines, nothing more to be said
anyway—the last silence between words.

The last of the lasts that have already been.

The last kiss, the last touch, the last
image of arms at midnight
the last breath before

the last.

Anthony (Tony) S. Abbott ( 1935-2020) was recipient of the 2015
North Carolina Award for Literature from the State of North
Carolina, and is the author of eight books of poetry, two novels,
and four books of literary criticism. His book of poems, *The Angel
Dialogues* (Lorimer Press, 2014), was the recipient of honorable
mention in the 2015 Brockman-Campbell competition of the
North Carolina Poetry Society, and his 2011 book of poems, *If
Words Could Save Us*, was the co-winner in that same competition
in 2012. His acclaimed first novel, *Leaving Maggie Hope*, won the
Novello Award in 2003 and was published by Novello Press.

Tony was born in San Francisco and educated at the Fay
School in Southborough, Massachusetts, and Kent School in Kent,
Connecticut. He received his AB from Princeton University, magna
cum laude, in 1957. With the support of a Danforth Fellowship,
he received his AM from Harvard University in 1960 and his PhD
in 1962. An instructor in English at Bates College for three years
beginning in 1961, he joined the English Department at North
Carolina's Davidson College in 1964. He became Full Professor
in 1979 and was named Charles A. Dana Professor of English in
1990. He served as the Chair of the Department from 1989 to
1996. Modern Drama, creative writing, and literature and religion
his major fields of interest, he is the author of two critical studies,
Shaw and Christianity and The Vital Lie: Reality and Illusion in
Modern Drama.

In addition to his teaching, for which Davidson College honored
him in 1969 with the Thomas Jefferson Award and in 1997 with

the Hunter-Hamilton Love of Teaching Award, Tony also served as President of the Charlotte Writers Club, the North Carolina Writers Network, and the North Carolina Poetry Society.

His first volume of poems, *The Girl in the Yellow Raincoat*, was published by St. Andrews Press in 1989 and was nominated for the Pulitzer Prize. His second poetry collection, *A Small Thing Like a Breath* was published by St. Andrews Press in 1993, and his third, *The Search for Wonder in the Cradle of the World* in 2000. A fourth collection, *The Man Who*, received the Oscar Arnold Young Award and was published by Main Street Rag Publishing Company in 2005.

His 2003 novel, *Leaving Maggie Hope*, was followed by its sequel, *The Three Great Secret Things*, published in 2007 by Main Street Rag Publishing Company. He returned to poetry in 2009 with his *New and Selected Poems: 1989-2009*, published by Lorimer Press, which also published his next two poetry collections, *If Words Could Save Us* and *The Angel Dialogues*, mentioned at the outset of this biography. Tony died in hospice, surrounded by his family, on October 3, 2020, one week before his induction into the North Carolina Literary Hall of Fame. *Dark Side of North*, is his last collection of poems, published by Press 53 on January 7, 2021: Tony's birthday.

9 781950 413317